K

Stuart Weir

Marshall Pickering
An Imprint of HarperCollinsPublishers

Marshall Pickering is an Imprint of
HarperCollins*Religious*
Part of HarperCollins*Publishers*
77–85 Fulham Palace Road, London W6 8JB

First published in Great Britain
in 1996 by Marshall Pickering

3 5 7 9 10 8 6 4 2

A catalogue record for this book is
available from the British Library

ISBN 0 551 03029 1

Printed and bound in Great Britain by
Caledonian International Book Manufacturing Ltd, Glasgow

For my family, Lynne, Christine and Jonathan.

Contents

Contents

Introduction

My professional responsibilities as Co-Director of Christians in Sport involve contributing to our mission of reaching the world of sport for Christ. In Christians in Sport, we believe that sport, done with the right attitude, can bring glory to God as much as any other human activity. We believe that there need be no conflict between being a Christian and playing sport with all your heart.

If anyone was seeking a role model to exemplify being a Christian in sport, they could do no better than look to Kriss Akabusi. For approaching ten years, Kriss has been an inspiration to all who endeavour to stand for Christ in the world of sport. It is a privilege for me to have access to Kriss's life and to be able to write about it.

I would like to express my thanks to Christine Smith, formerly Editorial Director at Marshall Pickering, for the invitation to write this book.

Thanks to the Editor of *Athletics Weekly*, Nigel Walsh, for permission to quote from the magazine and for giving me access to back numbers, and to Elaine

Dunn for looking after me in their offices. I am also grateful to Eddie Kulukundis, publisher of the now defunct *Athletics Today*, for permission to quote from that magazine. Ted Harrison's 1991 biography of Kriss, *Kriss Akabusi on Track*, has been a point of reference for me during the writing of this book. I am also grateful to Ian Hodge for answering all my statistical questions.

Thanks to my family for all their support as I struggled to complete the manuscript. Thanks to Helen Nunn for typing part of the manuscript, and to the rest of the Christians in Sport team, Andrew, Graham, Steve, Julia, Katie, Bryan and Judith. Finally, thanks to Steve Pargeter for his constant availability to advise Christians in Sport on computing matters.

The Olympic Dream

It is 6 August 1992, in Barcelona. The final of the men's 400 metres hurdles is about to start. Kriss Akabusi is on his marks. It is the most important race of his career – the culmination of 10 years in international athletics. The next 47 seconds will determine whether Kriss's ambition to become an Olympic Champion will be realized.

The Olympics remain unique as a sporting event. Held every four years, the Olympic Games represent the pinnacle of sporting achievement. Athletes sacrifice everything in the preceding four-year period for the chance of winning a medal or even just for the honour of taking part. The Olympics, more than any other sporting event, have managed to find a place for the true amateur, the representative of the tiny nation alongside the millionaire superstar American sprinter. The Olympics also have an unrivalled pedigree.

The Olympic Games, which began in 776 BC in Greece, are the clearest expression of the origin of organized sport. The games gathered competitors together on one site and integrated sport into a wider festival. They were taken very seriously. In Sparta, youths were taken from their families and reared in austere conditions in preparation for combat, the fore-runner of the modern training camp!

The modern Olympic movement was revived in 1896, in Athens mainly through the influence of Baron Pierre de Coubertin, who had the encouragement of Pope Pius X. The first modern Olympics were a huge success. While the athletic standards were modest, the enthusiasm and good sportsmanship of the Greek spectators ensured the success of the event.

For the athlete who fails, the four-year wait for the next opportunity of an Olympic medal can seem like an eternity. What Kriss wrote in the *Guardian* Diary sums up the significance of the event:

> On your marks…four years of blood, sweat and tears all hang on the performance of this day. There is no room for error. No second chance.

Barcelona is Kriss Akabusi's third Olympics. He competed in Los Angeles in 1984 and in Seoul in 1988. He already has an Olympic silver medal. His collection includes Commonwealth, European and World Championship gold medals. Only the Olympic gold is needed to complete the set.

In the years from 1988 to 1992, Akabusi's stock has risen. As well as the medals he had collected, he is also ranked third in the world. However, Kriss is 33 – nearer 34 if the truth be known – can he continue to improve, or will age finally catch up with him? Certainly, this is his last chance at that elusive Olympic gold medal.

Everything that Kriss has done in 1992 was in preparation for 6 August 1992. The training, the self-discipline, the self-denial, all to be in prime condition in the first week in August. The programme of races has been carefully chosen to bring him to peak fitness at just the right time. Not to peak too early nor too late. If Kriss Akabusi is to gain an Olympic gold medal, it is now or never. These thoughts crowd in as he goes to his marks and seeks to focus all his energy and attention on the race ahead.

To be truthful, 1992 has not been a great season. So far, he has done little to set the world alight. In his own words: 'I had trained like a dog. I had made mistakes in training and the pre-Olympic races had not gone well.'

Kriss's final preparations have been in Monte Carlo, where training has gone well. He arrived in Barcelona on 29 July, ready to do the business, ready to rock and roll.

Barcelona is an inspired choice for the Games of the 25th Olympiad. A vibrant and colourful city, with spectacular architecture and the famous Ramblas promenade running down from the heart of the city to the port, which bustles with boats large and small. Towering over the port is Montjuic, at the top of which stands the Olympic Stadium. The steep climb up Montjuic each morning is made easier by the escalators – a luxury denied the marathon runners – and the slow descent after the day's competition is enlivened by the dancing fountains, accompanied by a fantastic music and light show.

Inside the stadium, the atmosphere is tremendous – even though the Spaniards have a habit of whistling and jeering false starts, and give Khalid Skah the rudest of responses after that controversial 10,000 metres. The Games are full of incident and accident – Gail Devers falling over the last barrier when leading the 100 metres hurdles, Carl Lewis's revenge in the long jump, the gold medals of Christie and Gunnell, the downfall of the three hottest favourites, Messrs Morcelli, Johnson and Bubka. This Olympics amply demonstrates the unpredictability of sport and how easy it is for the household name, the hot favourite, to have what Jimmy Connors calls 'a bad day at the office'.

The Olympic 400 metres hurdles consists of three races in five days – heat, semi-final and final. The first task is to make the final – not to fall at the first hurdle, so to speak. Forty-seven competitors run in seven heats on 3 August. Kriss wins his heat in 48.98. He wins his semi-final two days later in a much quicker time of 48.01. Winthrop Graham wins the other semi-final in 47.62, with Kevin Young second, also under 48 seconds.

This is Kriss's assessment of his work so far:

When I went to the Olympic Games in 1992 I was expecting to get a medal. I had now had a lot of experience. I had become the best hurdler in Europe. So I went to the Barcelona Olympics with a real chance of picking up the Big G – the gold medal. In 1984 it had been enough to be there. In 1988 I was satisfied to make the final but in 1992 I felt that I had a real chance of winning the gold medal. As the Games started I got quite excited as I thought maybe I could win this time round. In the heats and the semi-final nobody looked that terrific.

The first goal has been accomplished, reaching the final. In the same Olympics, Jonathan Edwards, our number one triple jumper, has gone to Barcelona with high hopes of a medal. He has a disaster in the qualifying round and fails to make the final. In the semi-final of the men's 400 metres, Derek Redmond, the British record holder is running. Redmond had to pull out of the previous Olympics at the last minute with injury. In the last four years, he has undergone a succession of operations, mainly for Achilles tendon problems. In the 1991 World Championship he made no impact on the individual race but was in the historic UK 4 × 400 metres relay team which won the gold.

Now at last, for Redmond, it is beginning to happen. In the heat in Barcelona, he was flying. He starts well in the semi-final, then, after 150 metres, he pulls up sharply, clutching his hamstring. The Olympic dream is over. Minutes later, he is weeping inconsolably on trackside.

Kriss has avoided the pitfalls of injury and loss of form and has successfully made his way through to the 1992 Olympic final. He had gone to bed on 5 August knowing that all the preparation had been great, but now was the time to do the business. The athletes get to the stadium a couple of hours before the race. They go through their warm-up routines in the practice area. Then it is a case of waiting to be called to the track. The athletes set up their starting blocks, try them out, make any last-minute adjustments. Then it is time for business.

Kriss's own assessment was: 'On the day of the final, I was pretty excited – this was it – the finals had come! I got back to my marks and I was very confident actually. In the heats I had run particularly well and I felt very good and thought maybe I could win this time.' Kriss was not about to stand aside politely and let the favourites fight it out for the gold medal.

Kriss continues, 'The starter says, "Competitors on your marks." Your heart is pounding and you look around. For me, I always say a little prayer: "Well, Lord, here I am. I have prepared myself the best I can. Let's just do it." I'm thinking, "There's no ducking out now so let's just do it." That's the way I control and prepare myself.'

On your marks – Get set – Bang! The 1992 Olympic 400 metres hurdles final is under way! Kriss takes up the story:

I went as hard as I could but by the time I got to hurdle five the American, Kevin Young, came flying past me and I thought, 'Oh my gosh, I'm having a bad one.' At this point it would have been easy to panic – either to try to catch Young and burn myself out or to give up. Then as I got round the bend I worked really hard and I realized I wasn't running that bad because it was only Kevin Young who was ahead of me.

I got to the last hurdle late and Winthrop Graham came past me as well, but by the last 100 metres I knew that if I didn't make any mistakes I was going to hold on to my bronze medal. I think by the time I got to hurdle 10 that's all I was thinking about – holding on to my bronze medal – rather than wanting to catch anybody else.

I had been very confident in the final but it did not go according to plan, for one man ran a fantastic race. Even though I broke the British record yet again, Kevin Young broke the world record. Then I realized that for me the game was over. I did not expect to lose to a world record. I never expected Edwin Moses' record to be broken in my generation. I couldn't believe it! But in the end, as history records, I came third and now I'm very happy that I came third and got a medal.

That race was undoubtedly one of the highlights of the 1992 Olympics. While the race belonged to Kevin Young, who smashed the world record of the great Ed Moses on his way to the gold medal, Kriss still ran faster than ever before in his life. To crown a great career with an Olympic medal and another British record was a tremendous achievement. As Kriss often puts it when talking about the race, 'That day proved that I could not be the best. I had to be satisfied with just doing my best.' He adds, 'Kevin Young and I had one thing in common that day. His gold medal and my bronze each represented the best that we could be in our field of expertise.'

Despite his disappointments, Kriss had let no one down. To return home from the Olympic Games with one bronze medal, let alone two, made him the envy of the vast majority of the competitors. He could approach his retirement with contentment.

2

Early Life

In May 1955 a ship set sail from Lagos in West Africa bound for Liverpool. On board was a young Nigerian girl, Clara Adams, who was on her way to England to study as a nurse. There was, on the ship, another Nigerian, Kambi Duru Daniel Akabusi, who was on his way to study international law and accountancy at the University of London. Daniel and Clara met on the ship and spent some time together on the voyage. By the time they arrived in England, Daniel was most impressed with Clara, and kept in touch by letter and telephone. When Clara finished her nursing finals the couple were married.

On Friday 28 November 1958, their first baby was born. They named him Kezie Uche Chukwu Duru Akabusi. He is now better known as Kriss.

Kriss's early life was, by anyone's standards, difficult. That said, Kriss will dismiss such a suggestion with a shrug, saying, 'My life is my life,' and pointing out the positive benefits in later life that he gained from some of the early experiences.

The first three years of his life involved a succession of nannies and foster parents as both his parents pursued their careers. During that time, Kriss's younger brother, Riba, was born. In 1961, Daniel and Clara, having completed their studies, returned to Nigeria.

However, it was at that time a common practice among West African parents to believe that a British education would give their children an advantage. As a result, many West African parents sent their children to England to live with foster parents and receive English schooling. And so it was that when Kriss was approximately five, his mother brought him and Riba back to England and left them with a foster·mother in Brighton. Kriss's memories of this period are of strict discipline and regular beatings for him and Riba. Kriss recalled this period of his early life as follows:

> My brother and I learned, very young, that we must cling together and fight for our survival. We were the only constant thing in each other's lives. I'm not quite sure how old we were when our mother brought us from Nigeria to London to be fostered, but I am sure I was less than five and Riba not yet three.
>
> I remember standing outside our first foster home in Brighton, realizing, without quite understanding, that we were not going to see our mother again. There was an old lady who didn't care for us much. She had a son who abused us. It was an unhappy time but then I think she died and we were moved on.

We were moved so many times my memory is of being torn away from people I had become fond of and I learned never to let myself feel secure or that this was really home. I didn't even have a favourite toy to take with me. I coped as children do, but I can see now that it has had a lasting effect. Everyone thinks I'm so outgoing and make friends easily, but the truth is I don't let anyone really close to me. I have very few intimate friends and even with my wife, whom I love and value very much, I hold something back. I learned very young that trusting people led to pain and I suppose I can't get over that.

Because I am older than Riba, I took on a paternal role a lot of the time, but there were times when my instinct for self-preservation was stronger. We lived for a while with a Spanish woman who beat us. I quickly realized that if I cried and begged her to stop I didn't get such punishment, but Riba was stubborn and wouldn't cry or show the reverence she wanted, so she would beat and beat him. I knew I should intervene but I didn't want more beatings so I kept quiet.

Later, the children moved to Southsea in Hampshire, where they had a much more pleasant experience of being fostered by a couple called Bert and Dorrien Morgan.

In the 1960s, Nigeria suffered from civil war, involving the setting up of the short-lived independent state of Biafra. One of the results of this unsettled period in Nigeria was that communication with the outside world was difficult. As a result, the Morgans lost touch with Clara and Daniel Akabusi.

The next port of call for the Akabusi boys was a children's home on Village Road in Enfield which was to be their home for the next eight years, after the two boys had been found wandering around King's Cross. Kriss's memories of the circumstances are a bit hazy:

> We had been put on a train and told that when we got to the station at the other end someone would be there to meet us. We had been given two bars of chocolate and I had the Bournville dark chocolate because I knew Riba hated that. So we shared his chocolate and then when we came to my chocolate I got it all because he didn't like it. We were taken to the police station and after a while we were taken to the children's home in Enfield.

This event was very movingly dramatized as part of the BBC TV *Songs of Praise* programme in 1996.

> It was [in Enfield] that Riba began to shine at sports. He was far better than I was at everything and he was studious as well – his nose always in a book. I was busy making myself popular by messing about and being the clown of the class.

Of course we had scraps and rows at times, but when it mattered we were there for each other.

Kriss survived the time in the children's home without too many problems. He was popular at school, even if he did not make a great impact academically. As Kriss likes to put it, the only time he got glowing reports from school was when he set fire to them on the way home!

The early experiences of his life would have damaged many a person, but not Kriss. It is amazing how matter-of-fact he is when talking about his past, and how often he pulls a positive from the negative. For example, take this quotation from a 1991 interview with Mel Watman in *Athletics Today*:

My mother and father went back to Nigeria when I was three because they were sent over here on a scholarship to study – and so I wasn't in their plans, as it were... they decided it would be better to leave me with foster parents, to get a great education and go back to Nigeria when I was grown up. That was the idea. However, civil war broke out in 1967, when I was about eight, and the money they were sending for my upkeep stopped coming and so I was taken into child care.

I actually have good memories of child care really. I certainly had everything that I wanted, apart from intimacy. I had a few rough moments at a couple of foster homes but in the children's home they were pretty good to us. It was the intimate angle I missed; because when there are twenty children to look after no one can spare the time to really worry about you and your feelings, what's going through your life, or come to school and see your work and watch you run, and all those things.

But I did feel an inferiority in that wherever I went I had the stigma of coming from a children's home. So I always thought people were pointing their fingers at me; I always felt embarrassed to tell people I came from a children's home.

At school I was a wayward guy, always playing the clown, but I found that I could be good at sport and so I channelled all my abilities into my sport.

In sport he was keen but not outstanding. David Williams, the sports master at Edmonton School, is the unfortunate individual who once stated that 'Kriss has no athletic potential'! Kriss was second string runner for 400 metres, the school's best high jumper and played football for the 2nds.

Ted Harrison, in *Kriss Akabusi on Track*, quotes one of his teachers, Hugh Prosser, who said of Kriss that he was 'a memorable individual but also a constant irritant. He was continually naughty, though without being malicious.'

Kriss was aware, during this period, of being different from the average student in that he had no parents to take an interest in his progress. Kriss feels strongly now that it is very important to be at his children's sports days and open evenings and tries to arrange his schedule accordingly.

As a child he was irritated at being patronizingly referred to as 'the poor boy from the children's home'. On the positive side, this gave him a real determination to achieve something so that people could notice him and applaud him for being good at something, rather than pitying him as the poor boy from the children's home.

Over the years Kriss spent in the children's home, contact had been lost with his parents in Nigeria, although the International Social Services had constantly tried to re-establish contact. Out of the blue, in 1972, when Kriss was 13, a letter arrived from the ISS saying that contact had been made with both Kriss's parents. Correspondence ensued, especially with Clara, who enquired about the boys' progress. However, the re-establishment of contact with parents in a distant country made very little difference to Kriss.

Until his early teens, Kriss had been going fairly regularly to church. Then one particular Sunday he listened to the sermon and concluded that many of the things he enjoyed doing were deemed by the Church to be sinful. After giving the matter some thought, he prayed an unusual prayer that evening which went something like this: 'God, I don't know if you are out there, but I want to have a good time. I am still going to pray to you but I am not going to go to church.'

The prayer was interesting in two ways. It is notable that Kriss began the prayer with 'God, I don't know if you are out there...' because it was with a similar formulation that he later began the prayer in his room in California which led to his becoming a Christian (see Chapter 5). Having a good time has remained high on his agenda, yet when he spoke at the Billy Graham mission at Crystal Palace in 1989, he finished with the words, 'Guys – I had a good time before I was a Christian but I've had a better time ever since.' The perception of the teenage boy that God had to prove himself and to be able to make a better offer than anyone else didn't change much as Kriss moved into adulthood.

In 1975, Kriss's mother paid a visit to England and came to meet him. He recalls his attitude to the meeting as being one of curiosity but not any real excitement.

I can remember seeing her arrive at the children's home. I was playing football in the garden. I looked up and instantly recognized who she was. She was dressed in traditional Nigerian dress. I could feel no bonding or natural affection. I had lots of friends who had mothers. To stop and think, 'Hang on! This is your mother!' was a very strange sensation. It wasn't a case of long-lost son – tears and all that. It was more a case of looking at each other, and realizing she was my mother.

He found it difficult to establish any close bond to a person he had not seen for 12 years. Clara Akabusi wanted Kriss and Riba to return to Nigeria with her, but Kriss was not impressed with this suggestion. England was the only country that he knew and that was where he wanted to stay.

> When I saw my mother in all her Nigerian clothes it increased my phobia about the country. When she said she wanted to take me back to Nigeria with her, I just clung on to my chair and said, 'No, I am not going.'

One effect of his mother's visit was to remind Kriss of his Nigerian background and heritage, although this remained for the moment at the back of his mind.

Kriss was certain he wanted to stay in England, but other questions remained to be decided. Brian Martin, who ran the children's home, shared with Kriss his own good experiences from the Army. He told Kriss that there were great opportunities for sport and that he could learn a trade. At the time, Kriss was thinking about being a motor-mechanic or a gas-fitter, but the Army seemed a more interesting prospect.

As Kriss entered his last year at school and in the children's home, he was gradually coming to the conclusion that the Army was where his immediate future should be. Having lived all his life to this point in an institution, joining another would be an easy transition. The alternative of establishing himself independently – finding a job, somewhere to live, etc. – was a much more daunting prospect. On the down side it would have been reasonable to question whether the impulsive and ill-disciplined teenage Akabusi would survive the rigours of army life. But, as Kriss puts it, the Army offered him somewhere to live, something to eat, and clothes to wear – 'OK, the clothes were green, but you can't have everything.'

After an interview with the recruitment officer and a series of aptitude tests, Kriss was offered a place in the British Army and an apprenticeship in data telegraphy. On 7 August 1975, he took himself to the Army recruitment office in Finchley and signed the necessary forms.

On 9 September 1975, Kriss boarded a train at King's Cross station, heading for Newcastle. His ultimate destination was Albemarle Barracks at Ouston. In some ways, Kriss was struggling with his identity at this time. He had certainly decided that England was his home, yet was aware of his Nigerian heritage. He was aware of being black in a predominantly white society. The name Kezie Akabusi certainly betrayed a non-English origin. To counter this, he decided to change his name to Kriss. That he decided on Kriss, rather than Chris, was an indication both of his extrovert personality and the desire, even if he was going to be English, to be a little bit different. No common or garden 'Chris' for him!

3

In the Army Now

Joining the Army was a turning point for Kriss in more ways than one. In some ways it was an easy option. Kriss also saw it as a challenge and an opportunity. As he put it years later:

> I joined the Army at sixteen out of social conditioning. I was institutionalized. It was the only environment I felt comfortable in. Bed, meals, clothes provided. Sports, travel and trade guaranteed. Recipe made in heaven. I changed my name. This was going to be a clean break from the past. No more failure at school, no social outcast from the children's home. This was my first opportunity to show what I could do on merit. I would show everyone I was their equal.

On the very first day in the Army Kriss lined up on the parade square with eight hundred other young men. As Kriss likes to tell it,

> They then brought out this machine called a sergeant-major. He came out and started shouting

commands to the soldiers: 'Att-en-tion!' He said, 'There are eight hundred men on parade but by the end of the twenty-eighth week of training some will be sick and some will have gone home to mama.'

Those words struck a chord with Kriss, as he explains:

When he said that I determined that I would not be one of those who went home to mama. Now the fact that I didn't have a mama to go home to didn't matter. Each week he read out the list of the sick and the lazy and those who had gone home to mama. At the end of the twenty-eight weeks the sergeant-major lined us up and bellowed, 'There are now four hundred men on parade. Two hundred have gone sick. One hundred are lame and one hundred have gone home to mama.'

That was a very special day for Kriss. As he stood there as one of the four hundred who had made it, the boy from the children's home, the boy who left school branded as a failure, knew that for the first time in his life he had achieved something. He had stuck at something and seen it through to completion.

Later in life, Kriss would quote the Book of Proverbs, chapter 29 verse 18: 'People with no vision perish'. He comments: 'I found that to be true in my life. I realized that the things I wanted to accomplish, the things I wanted to do could not be achieved without having a goal to go for, without persevering and really working hard at something I would fall short of the mark.' Already in the early days of his army career, he was discovering that.

Getting up at 5.30 a.m. was a bit of a shock to the system for Kriss, but by 6.30 the young soldiers had to be up, washed, dressed with have their dorm tidied for inspection. By 9.00 – the time he would normally have been arriving at school – he felt as if he'd already done half a day's work.

Another difference was that Kriss found he was able to apply himself in the classes in a way that he never could at school. The motivation to succeed in the data telegraphist course pushed him to give his best in everything. At his passing out ceremony in April 1976, Junior Signalman Akabusi was justifiably proud of his achievements. His reports described him as 'a hard-working, cheerful and reliable soldier'. His team spirit and physical stamina were listed as 'outstanding' with determination, self-confidence and ambition 'above average'. In all subjects he was graded average or better.

This is Kriss's own assessment of his army experience thus far:

When you join the Army you soon learn discipline and in a way it was an environment in which I thrived. I did well, and I found that in education classes too I could compete with the others purely because – unlike at school – I couldn't mess about. If I messed about I would be charged or have money deducted or be put on duties.

I began to gain a little more self-discipline and ambition. Previously I had just wanted to play the fool; now I wanted to be a lance-corporal, I wanted to be a good soldier. I matured very fast. (Mel Watman interview in *Athletics Today*)

Having completed his initial training, Kriss was then assigned to Catterick in North Yorkshire to begin his training in data telegraphy, where he learned to type, operate a teleprinter and a tape relay machine, as well as how to decipher codes.

The next thing on the agenda was an overseas posting. He was sent to Lippstadt in Germany to join 22 Signal Regiment. So it was that in early 1977 he found himself at Luton Airport on a plane to Germany, his first flight since coming back from Nigeria as a child.

Kriss's first six months at Lippstadt proved to be somewhat boring, with not a lot to do. Moreover, he found little opportunity to use his newly acquired skills in data telegraphy. A turning point came when a fellow soldier invited Kriss to accompany him to a local disco. Among the girls he met at the disco was an attractive blonde called Monika. She admits that at first it was Kriss's red sports car more than Kriss himself that attracted her!

The friendship developed, and affected Kriss in more ways than one. Ultimately, Monika was to become his wife. In the short term, they discovered a common interest in sport and physical fitness. Monika says, 'Kriss was the guy to be with. He was the main extrovert. He would get on the floor and dance and dance. He was very good.'

By this stage, Kriss had become an army physical training instructor. Every soldier was expected to maintain a certain degree of physical fitness and it was Kriss's job to administer tests to ensure that they did so. He had also progressed to the rank of lance-corporal.

When it was first suggested to Kriss that he should aim to become a PTI, he was unsure. He doubted if he was good enough. A colleague assured him that he was and also offered to give him any help he needed. Without that encouragement he would probably not have gone for it. However, it proved to be just what he needed.

Kriss was later to acknowledge the contribution of the Army to the development of his athletics career, at this stage:

> At twenty-four, when a lot of people may have decided to hang up their boots, I carried on. I was fortunate in that I was in the Army, and the Army gave me a lot of backing at that time in my career, whereas a lot of guys of twenty-four who haven't broken 48 seconds for 400 metres have to start worrying about their wife and kids. (Mel Watman interview in *Athletics Today*)

Kriss also acknowledges another contribution that the Army made to his athletics career: 'It helped me keep my feet on the ground – one minute you were a track star and the next just another soldier doing his job.'

The visit to the children's home by his mother had kindled his interest in Nigeria, and at the age of 19 he made a trip to the country. He was amazed at the welcome he got at his father's village. There was a 21-gun salute, women dancing and singing songs. This all went on for a couple of hours. As news spread that Chief Akabusi's son was paying a visit, people started coming with chicken, goats, and other livestock for him.

They also came with kola nuts – a ceremonial nut to be shared among men. They came with their blessings and their wisdom to welcome him back to the village. However, as Kriss recalls, it did not all go smoothly:

> One thing that distressed me is that I am a very playful character. I was used to messing around in the children's home and as a junior soldier. In the village I tried to do the same but that was frowned on. I wasn't supposed to mix with the people. I was supposed to act the educated foreigner. They wanted to see me in my suit, speaking properly. I was expected to present myself as a well-educated westerner, the Chief's son, but instead I was messing around with the children.

Kriss then spent a period in Aldershot, improving his qualifications and becoming a Sergeant in the Physical Training Corps. His next assignment was as Sergeant Instructor with the Gloucester Regiment. As a PT instructor, he was responsible for organizing and supervising courses in Battle PT, designed to keep experienced servicemen in prime condition.

Spending so much time in England may have helped the development of his career but it did little for his relationship with Monika. They saw each other only when they could afford to fly back and forward, and when holidays permitted. In late 1981 Kriss decided that the friendship with Monika was going nowhere. He telephoned her and said, 'It's over. It's been great but things have moved on.'

Rather than accept this, Monika got on the next flight to England and presented herself at Kriss's door. Kriss realized that if Monika was willing to drop everything and come straight to see him, then she was a bit special. He looked her straight in the eye and said, 'OK, we'll give it a try.'

Monika replied, 'So we'll get married?'

Kriss responded, 'Well, yes, OK, why not?'

As Ted Harrison put it, it was 'hardly the romantic proposal of the century', but it did the trick. Kriss and Monika were married at the Register Office in Salisbury on 2 April 1982.

Kriss had begun to race in Army championships in 1976, and for many years his ambitions as an athlete did not go beyond becoming Army Champion or Inter-Services Champion. By the mid-1980s, however, Kriss was competing successfully at the top level, and his army salary was no longer his only income. What is more, his army duties were at times in danger of getting in the way of his athletic training.

Early in 1989, Kriss asked for a leave of absence for twenty months to allow him to concentrate on working towards 1990 with its two major championships. The Army said no. The issue came to a head in 1989. While the Army was accommodating when it came to fitting in training, it still required him to do a job of work to earn his keep.

After the Commonwealth Games in 1990, Kriss wanted to train in California as part of his build-up to the summer season. The military authorities told him that they had a seven-week posting for him before he was free to concentrate on training.

Feeling that this would compromise his training, Kriss decided he must leave the Army and decided to buy himself out. His final release date was set for 13 December 1989. Then, suddenly, the Army reconsidered and made Kriss an offer. If he would stay on the Army pay-roll for another year and do a small amount of what might, in other walks of life, be called PR work, he would be free to train full-time during that year.

Kriss agreed. When a particular success in 1990 was described in the *Guardian* as 'a victory for the Army', the Army personnel who had made the decision must have been rubbing their hands with glee.

He left the Army in November 1990 after 15 years. It was right for more than one reason. As he said later: 'The Army publicity was all about security, learning a trade, seeing the world, and doing sport. As a teenager, I never realized it was where you actually learned to kill people.'

Kriss only began to understand this side of the Army when his unit was put on stand-by for service in the Falklands.

Even though I was afraid of getting shot and dying and didn't like the idea of killing people, I knew I was sufficiently trained to obey my orders, take my rifle and kill someone. It was then that I realized that principles can be subordinated to a sense of duty – I would willingly have died for my country. From that moment I knew the Army wasn't for me.

He summed up his military experience like this:

I came in as a boy, I leave as a man, and the self-discipline which I have gained will set me up for life. At the same time I believe it will greatly guide me in the next stage of my life. Yes, I do have trepidation as I will be leaving a system that has given me security, support and an alternative to thinking about track and field all the time.

He acknowledges, too, the legacy his time in the Army has left in his home life.

Being a military man I like to have things bang! bang! bang! I get annoyed if my wife parks her car on the left in the garage because I always park mine on the left!

The Army, too, was pleased with Warrant-Officer Akabusi. He had been the first soldier for 20 years to compete in an Olympic track event. Lieutenant-General Sir John Learmont said of him, 'We are extremely proud of the manner in which you have represented your country and the success you have achieved... You leave a marvellous example for others to follow.'

4

Discovering He Could Run

Kriss Akabusi's running career developed almost by chance. He had left school with the great encouragement of his games teacher's report: 'Akabusi has no talent for sport'.

One day, not long after he had entered the Army, Kriss joined Sergeant Ian Mackenzie on a training run around an airfield. Mackenzie was, by Army standards, a good runner. He and Kriss ran together for a bit, then, towards the end, Mackenzie accelerated, expecting to leave his young companion standing. However, Kriss sprinted with him and overtook him, leaving Mackenzie to shout: 'What do you think you are doing? I am supposed to be the fastest around here!'

As a result of this incident, Kriss found himself entered for an Army race. His reaction was to say: 'No, thank you, I don't want to run.'

The reply was typical of the Army ethos: 'Akabusi, I didn't ask you if you wanted to run. I was telling you that you were running. Is that clear?'

'Yes, sir,' was the only reply acceptable.

He won the race, a 400 metres. Before long he also won the Army Junior (under 18) Championship. That was 1976, and he was running the 400 metres in 52.4 seconds. The following year, he managed to improve to 49.1. In 1979, he ran 48.7, and at the age of twenty found himself, for the first time, in the official UK rankings of the top runners in his event. He was 56th.

In the winter of 1979, when stationed in Germany, he went to a local club and started training properly and his times improved next summer. It was then he realized for the first time that he might make something of himself as an athlete.

Kriss was, at this stage, winning Army races, but was not in regular training. Monika introduced him to the local athletics club, LG Gütersloh. He made an immediate impression on one of the top German coaches, Hansi Böhme, who told him that he had the potential to achieve things if he were to dedicate himself to running rather than continually turning up to training with injuries picked up in other sports.

Kriss heeded his advice and immediately reduced his personal best from 50.3 seconds to 48.0 seconds. This got him into some of the better races in Germany where the crowds numbered between three and five thousand.

In 1979, Kriss attended his first warm-weather training camp in Bolzano in the Northern Italian Alps. One significant thing happened there.

I picked up a quote from Alexander Pope, the English poet from the Age of Reason: 'Blessed are they who expect nothing for they will not be disappointed'. I wrote this down in my training diary and determined that this would be my approach to winning in athletics.

In 1980, with a time of 48.0, he had moved up to 32nd in the rankings. However, to put it in context, David Jenkins, the British number one, had a best of 45.29 that season. Kriss made no real progress during the next two years. At that stage, aged almost 24 and not in the top 30 in the country, there was nothing to suggest that Kriss would ever be more than just a good club and county runner.

The turning point came when he decided to transfer from the Royal Signals to the Army Physical Training Corps. Mike Smith, a leading athletics coach, came up from Southampton to speak to an athletics coaching course and asked Kriss to join his squad, which included Todd Bennett. He readily accepted the invitation.

Immediately, Kriss found himself on a tougher regime than he had ever experienced before, with much harder training. The new training methods bore immediate results.

Kriss is in no doubt about the importance of Mike Smith's input at this stage:

I'm quite sure I would have carried on running 48 seconds for a very long time if I had not gone to see Mike. In Germany they were very technically orientated and I had spent a lot of time doing drills and running tall and being technically sound, but they neglected the speed/endurance

aspect. Under Mike Smith it was totally different. In Mike's group we didn't do as much work
technically, we didn't break down the movement
and do all the various drills, but we did lots of
hard work. (Mel Watman interview in *Athletics
Today*)

In fact when Kriss received his MBE in 1991 for his
services to athletics, Mike Smith was in his thoughts.

Receiving the MBE was nice, but think about
someone like Mike Smith who works so hard.
He has dedicated forty years of his life to British
athletics; he has coached twelve or more top
British athletes. His contribution to British athletics was far greater than mine but I am the guy
who gets the recognition.

Kriss found himself doing cross-country and road runs
to build up his stamina, and sessions of up to two
hours on circuits in the gym to increase his power.
When the summer came and they ventured on to the
track, it was serious, planned work not just running
laps. It was 200 or 300 metre runs, repeated six or
eight times with short periods of recovery in between.

It paid dividends the following summer. He
entered the 1983 season with a personal best of 48
seconds and a ranking in the 30s'. He ended it almost
two seconds faster at 46.10, a British International,
and even found himself selected for the UK relay
team in the World Championships in Helsinki.

The 1983 season started with second place in the UK Championships, running a personal best of 46.85. The excitement of the achievement faded a little on the journey home when he was stopped for speeding on the motorway, resulting in a £60 fine.

All of a sudden he found himself ushered into top flight athletics, being selected for Great Britain v. USSR in Birmingham on 5 June 1983. He remembers rushing home and showing Monika and Mike Smith his selection letter from Frank Dick. It was to be the first of many. He came fourth in the race in a not too distinguished time.

Two weeks later he was running for Britain again, this time in Finland, where he won in the race with another personal best of 46.81. He finished the season in Oslo with a brilliant 46.10 to win an international race and beat Phil Brown for the first time.

Two more significant international appearances put the icing on the cake in Kriss's first season of international competition. He was selected for the 4 × 400 metres relay in the Europa Cup, a team competition, at Crystal Palace. He ran the first leg and Britain won the race.

The World Championships must have seemed light-years away when Kriss started the season, yet that is where he was headed in August 1983.

The 1983 World Championships are probably best remembered for Carl Lewis's four gold medals – 100 metres, 200 metres, 4 × 100 metres and the long jump. Kriss was there as a junior member of the 4 × 400 metres relay squad. He ran in the heats and semi-finals but was not selected for the final, and Ainsley Bennett, Garry Cook, Todd Bennett and Phil Brown gained the World Championship bronze medal. Because Kriss had run in the two qualifying races, the British team made a special representation to the IAAF and an extra bronze medal was provided for Kriss.

The significance of the 1983 season was also that Kriss moved from being a soldier whose hobby was running to an international athlete whose job happened to be the Army. With an Olympic season looming, the Army considered Kriss's position and decided that he should be posted to Marchwood in Hampshire, to be near to his coach, Mike Smith. The Army also decided that, as far as possible, Kriss's army duties should not interfere with his preparations for the Olympics.

As the 1984 season began, Kriss knew that the Olympics were well within his grasp if he could but regain his form of the previous season. He started in great form, equalling his personal best in winning the UK Championships in Cwmbran. The following week, he broke 46 seconds for the first time (45.85) but could only finish third behind Todd Bennett and Phil Brown.

It was enough to confirm his Olympic selection, conveyed to him in a personally signed letter from the Duke of Edinburgh. He was on his way to the Olympics in Los Angeles!

The experience of the 1984 Olympics was magic for Kriss. Just to be there was the fulfilment of a dream in itself. He recalls:

I had never been to America before but I had read all the boys' comics and I was very excited about going to see Spiderman. My first impression was how friendly the Americans were: 'Hey man, how are you doing? That's neat!' and so on. It really was a dream come true.

He ran in the 400 metres. Kriss was there as the third string British runner, behind Todd Bennett and Phil Brown. However, in the first and second heats he did personal bests including in 45.43, the second fastest ever by a Briton. He was the only Briton to progress to the semi-finals.

He came seventh in the semi-final, in 45.69. How far Kriss was off the pace is shown by the Alonzo Babers's gold medal-winning time of 44.27, a full 1.16 seconds faster than his own personal best.

Looking back on the event, Kriss now feels that his inexperience was a major factor in his semi-final performance. He was over the moon about the personal best in the previous round. He was in a 'go out and enjoy it' frame of mind. The more professional Akabusi of later in his career would have been totally focused on getting in the top four to make the final.

He recognizes, too, that he was a bit 'gobsmacked' by the whole Olympic experience, and that his attitude to the 1988 and 1992 games was much more professional.

When you go to the Olympics every four years, you see people you have not seen for a long time.

You meet people from all over the world and the one thing you have in common is that you are all good sportsmen, for the Olympic Games are the meet of champions. There is a friendship, there is a camaraderie, but in the last analysis it is all about competition. You are all friendly and dining together but when your event is approaching you become channelled, very focused on the event ahead. In a way there is a distinction between the first-time Olympian who is soaking up the atmosphere and the experienced guys who want to do everything right to try to make the medal rostrum. They have been preparing all year – and longer – just for one moment.

The 4 × 400 metres relay in Los Angeles brought Kriss an unexpected silver medal. While none of the rest of the team had even matched Kriss's achievement of reaching the semi-final of the individual 400 metres, let alone the final, they worked as a team. Kriss (running the first leg), Garry Cook, Todd Bennett and Phil Brown came second in a new British record time of 2:59.13.

Prior to this race, only two relay teams had ever run under 3 minutes. On this occasion, the Australians ran 2:59.7 only to get fourth place. In what the 1985 International Running Guide referred to as a 'cracking final', Britain were in fourth place with half a lap to go when Phil Brown overtook first the Australians and then the Nigerians to grab the silver medal position. The performance was a good example of what Kriss calls 'the whole being greater than the sum of the parts', meaning that there are times when a team working together can exceed what would be the sum total of their individual achievements.

It was Kriss's first experience – the first of many – of getting a medal at a major championship. To stand on the rostrum and receive an Olympic medal and to be acclaimed for your achievement is, indeed, a magic moment.

The 1984 Olympics were an important step on the ladder for Kriss. He had gone to the Olympics as an athlete. In Los Angeles he had become an Olympian. What is more, he had come back with a silver medal, more than the majority of athletes ever achieve.

It was a very satisfying Olympic debut for Kriss. Two personal bests had been achieved in his individual event and his contribution to the relay team had helped secure a silver medal. He comments,

Pierre de Coubertin, the founder of the modern Olympic Games, said, 'The important thing in the Olympic Games is not to win but to take part; the important thing in life is not the triumph but the struggle; the essential thing is not having conquered but to have fought well.'

However, I was soon to learn the folly of these words in the modern era. I won a silver medal in the British relay quartet and made the semi-final as an individual. I certainly had not expected the silver and had only hoped that I would make the semis. I was ecstatic with jubilation.

On my return home I was to learn from experience a cruel truth. In world class sport, winning is everything. Coming second means nothing. Marketing managers and PR officers want winners; sponsors and advertisers want winners; armchair critics and enthusiastic punters want winners. 'Win, win, win,' say the media moguls, 'and we will make you stars.' Sport, I realized, was definitely more than a game.

When he broke into top level athletics, Kriss was told by people that he must be very careful never to cross Andy Norman, the British Athletics promotions officer, or his opportunities to run would be reduced. Kriss was not impressed. He decided that he was not going to bow and scrape to anyone and that he would take his chances to be accepted into meets on his merits, not because he appeased Mr Norman.

I suppose I had a love/hate relationship with Andy Norman. I think in the end we respected each other. I need to have control of my own life so there was always going to be a clash with Andy. When I first met him, I remember thinking, 'There is no way you are going to control my life'. He wanted to tell me where I was going to run, where I could and could not run. That was never going to work with me. In the end I think he respected me because I was prepared to stand up to him and I respected him because he called a spade a spade.

Any anger I had at Andy, I used positively. If I felt annoyed with him it made me more determined to succeed and to do so well that he would have to have me running whether he wanted to or not. I think he respected me for that.

A year or two after I retired I met Andy at a dinner, sat next to him and we got on fine. For all his faults you look at British Athletics now and you conclude that it needs an Andy Norman. He was a wheeler and dealer but he was the best.

Similarly, Kriss was aware that some athletes were very concerned not to upset the national coach, Frank Dick. Kriss had no wish to be on bad terms with anyone but, again, he was not prepared to bite his lip if he felt that things needed to be said about the organization of British athletics. Again he had the confidence that if his times were good enough he would be selected to run for Britain. Perhaps his separate army life gave him an independence that most other athletes did not have.

Another significant event in 1984 was the birth of a daughter to Monika and Kriss; Ashanti arrived on 19 June 1984 in Berlin, where Kriss had been posted for part of that year.

1985 saw Kriss making no real progress. In 1984 he had run three personal bests, but in 1985 he was unable to improve on the previous year's effort. 1985 was also a quiet year, with no major championship taking place. He ran 45.56 to win in Madrid and 45.55 in a heat of the AAA championship, only to finish fifth in the final next day in a much slower time. On the international scene, he ran for Britain in the 4×400 metres relay in the Europa Cup final.

Never mind that 1985 was a quiet year. He probably needed it to recover from the dramatic increase in status of the past two years. In any case, 1986, with its European Championships and Commonwealth Games, would certainly make up for it.

5

Times of Change

Kriss Akabusi knew that 1986 was going to be an important year. It offered two major championships, the Commonwealth Games and the European Championships; two chances to see if he could establish himself on the world stage. However, he had no real clue at the beginning of 1986 just how significant the year would be or that he would make two decisions that year which would be literally life-changing.

He started with a win in a race at Walnut, California, in a respectable time of 45.74 (against his personal best of 45.43, set in 1984). Following that, he came only fourth in the UK Championships in 45.65, which would prove to be his best time in 1986, finishing behind Phil Brown (45.29), Brian Whittle and Roger Black. In the AAA championships he was third in 46.08, behind Darren Clark (44.94) and Roger Black (45.16).

It was not the form he would have liked, perhaps, but it got him selected for the Commonwealth Games in Edinburgh in the 400 metres and relay. He just missed a medal in the Commonwealth Games 400 metres, coming fourth in 46.83. Roger Black won in

45.57 from Darren Clark of Australia (45.98), with Phil Brown third in 46.80. Kriss had won his semi-final in 47.55, beating both Clark and Brown.

England (Akabusi, Roger Black, Todd Bennett and Phil Brown) took the gold medal in the 4 x 400 metres relay. However, that the winning time was 3:07.19 was an indication of the relatively poor standard of the race. Running as Great Britain, more or less the same team was to run over seven seconds faster in the European Championships later in the month. Nonetheless, it was a first major championship gold medal for Kriss – another landmark. On their lap of honour, the team stopped to bow to the Queen, Prince Philip and Prince Edward who were in the royal box.

Kriss had gone to the Commonwealth Games in 1986 with a lot on his mind. In his own words, he 'was thinking a lot about life'. He had questions in his mind:

> I had everything going for me. I had a good job, I had a nice house, a flash car, a lovely wife and family but somehow I felt there was something missing. A few situations had gone on in my life that had stopped me in my tracks and made me think: 'What is life all about?'

At that stage he had a very materialistic view of life. 'I felt that the purpose of life was to see who could die with the most toys.'

One toy was his car. He admits that since he was a boy, he always wanted a Mercedes-Benz car. When he managed to afford his first Mercedes, he thought it was perfect. Until, that is, one day when he was cruising along in his Mercedes and someone overtook him in a bigger Mercedes! He wanted the bigger one.

One particular incident had caused Kriss to stop and think. His wife Monika gave birth to stillborn twins. The experience profoundly affected him.

> I had expected to see a foetus but instead I saw two small dolls with all their features perfect except that they had a goose-pimply type skin. It looked as if they were sleeping. When the twins were born dead I was thinking where have they gone to? Is this it? It really got me thinking about where do we come from? Where are we going to?
>
> I was running very well and had fame and fortune but there was nothing there when I got there. My wife had twins and then lost them and I just thought, 'What is the point of life?'

At the Commonwealth Games, the National Bible Society of Scotland had placed a Bible in every competitor's room. In many ways, a major championship is quite a boring time for the competitors. They train for an hour or so each day, but what do they do the rest of the time? Everything is geared to the event, so one does not want to waste energy, physical or emotional, on anything which could be a distraction from the matter in hand. Rest is the order of the day.

Kriss could hardly have found a Bible at a better time. He was looking for something to occupy him so he opened the Bible, found it was a modern translation, the Good News translation of the New Testament. He started reading it and just carried on. By the end of the two weeks in Edinburgh, he had finished reading it!

This is how he summed up his first reaction:

It was the Good News Bible and it was good news for me for I could actually understand it. The only Bible I had seen before was full of 'thees' and 'thous' and whatnot – words that I could not understand. I read the Bible and in it I met a guy. His name was Jesus.

I was familiar with the name of Jesus. I was used to hearing it in the school playground and in the Army – Jesus this and Christ that! What I had not grasped was that this Jesus had been a real person and that he had actually lived on earth. That got me thinking about the claims he made. For example: 'I have come that they may have life, and have it to the full' (John 10:10), or 'I am the way and the truth and the life. No one comes to the Father except through me' (John 14:6).

I was really excited about what I read and thought, 'Wouldn't it be nice if I could really live the kind of life this guy wants to offer me?' But I had that niggling feeling that it could be like Father Christmas and the tooth fairy – not real. But it didn't give me any peace.

Kriss left Edinburgh deeply impressed by this Jesus and determined to find out more about him. Over the next few months he read a great deal to find out if Jesus of Nazareth really was who he said he was – the Son of God. Gradually, he found that there were answers to the questions he was asking. Everything convinced him that this Jesus was someone to be taken seriously.

However, he did not have much time to think about it just at the moment. Scarcely had he come home from the Commonwealth Games and changed his socks before he was off to Stuttgart for the European Championships. To his disappointment, he was not selected for the individual 400 metres. To add insult to injury, he was named only as reserve for the relay team. With Roger Black winning the individual 400 metres flat gold medal and Derek Redmond, aged twenty, coming fourth, the British selectors were justified in their selection, although Kriss would have expected to do better than Phil Brown's eighth in the semi-final.

And, talking of injury, he had picked up a niggle in his hamstring between the Commonwealth and the European Championships. The role of injured reserve – or 'baggage-man', as Kriss described it – was not very appealing. However, in the event, he was fit, and an injury to Todd Bennett got Kriss into the team and a relay gold medal.

In the European Championship relay, Kriss sensed an 'awareness of God':

I was injured but I knew that if I pulled out, the whole team would lose, so I prayed and read the Bible. I read about putting your faith in the Lord – if you have the faith of a mustard seed you can move mountains. I said to myself as I warmed up, 'You are all right, God is with you.'

I got to 120 metres and started to feel my leg. The niggling pain came right back but I told myself to have faith. I kept on running and won a gold medal.

As Kriss approached his twenty-eighth birthday he reflected on where he was athletically. After the early years of progress, he had hit a plateau. He had not been able to improve on the personal best he set in the Los Angeles Olympics in the two years since that event. He should have been at his peak now. In reality, he was at a crossroads, unsure of whether he had a future in international athletics.

At 28, he certainly wasn't past his sell-by date, yet if he could no longer be sure of a place in the team for major championships – even for the relay – the question about his future had to be asked. In his own inimitable way he told himself, 'You're a cart-horse, Kriss. You're just a 45.5 man and in the future that's not going to be good enough even to make the relay team.'

Faced with the same evidence, others would have drawn different conclusions. Some would have deluded themselves into thinking that they were better than they really were, that their prospects were OK and that they would improve. Others would be content with what had been achieved so far – the international bests, the Olympic silver medal in the relay, etc. Kriss, in contrast, made a decision and had the determination to follow it through.

He faced the issue with total honesty and ruthless logic. His analysis went like this:

Fact 1   He had been unable to improve his time for the past two seasons. Perhaps he had reached the height of his achievement.

Fact 2   Alongside the established 400 metres runners like Todd Bennett, Ainsley Bennett and Phil Brown, younger men of great potential were appearing on the scene, for example Derek Redmond and Roger Black.

Fact 3   In the 400 metres hurdles, Britain had no outstanding competitor. (In the recent European Championships, the best two Britons, Phil Beattie and Max Robertson, had each come seventh in their semi-finals, neither breaking 50 seconds.) David Hemery's British record had stood for 18 years.

Kriss put these three facts into the melting pot, gave it a good stir and decided that his future lay over the hurdles.

I came to the conclusion that if I continued as a 400 metres (flat) runner, Stuttgart would be my last major championship. Never again would I run in front of a huge crowd and enjoy that special atmosphere. My rivals were young. I could see the next squad coming along and I was out of it. But watching the British guys in the hurdles in the European Championships, there was nobody special. I believed I could make the British team as a hurdler.

Roger Black, Kriss's great friend, commented, 'It's his greatest quality – he's a total realist.'

There was one other alternative – and Kriss did consider it – drugs.

I got to a position where I wondered if I had reached my full potential. I wondered if the only way forward was to take performance-enhancing drugs. My saving grace was that I didn't know where to go to get them. Also, as I weighed up the pros and cons, I realized that if I was caught, not only would my athletics career go down the pan but so would my military career. More importantly, I worried about the effect on my family and decided that it probably wasn't a good idea.

While at the European Championships, Kriss approached Peter Warden about wanting to become a hurdler. On his return home he drove up to Manchester to train with Max Robertson and a few others. After three weekly journeys to Manchester – a five hundred-mile round trip – he realized that he needed a coach who was much nearer. Mike Smith suggested Mike Whittingham.

Kriss approached Mike Whittingham, a former international hurdler who was now coaching. Whittingham instantly recognized Kriss's potential. Did he think he had a future champion?

I have to say yes. I sat down and listened, for Kriss had already decided where he wanted to go and what he wanted to do. First he wanted to be number one in Britain and then he wanted to set his sights on the European Championships in 1990. I thought that was a good target since it was over three years away and it gave him enough time to learn to hurdle and to improve a bit each year.

Kriss asked me, 'What do you think my potential is?' Now it isn't every day that you are approached by a 400 metre runner who has already run 45.5, who was incredibly dedicated to hard work and to learning a new skill. In view of this I said, 'You have the potential to break the British record.'

Whittingham recognized that underneath the sunny character and the happy-go-lucky exterior there was a competitive spirit second to none.

During an early race, Kriss was doing well until he hit the ninth hurdle and fell flat on his face on the track. He recalls the incident well. 'In that moment I could have got up and said, "No thanks, this isn't for me," but instead I got up and was more determined than ever that I would work harder until I was successful.'

Mike Whittingham warned Kriss that it would take a great deal of hard work. That didn't frighten Kriss. As Mike Whittingham says of him, 'Kriss has lifted himself by sheer effort from being a good club athlete to being an international runner.'

Kriss started a rigorous series of leg exercises and drills. He started to clear small hurdles, constantly improving and developing his hurdling technique. In the early days, Kriss worked with Mike twice a week.

Early in 1987 he went to America for warm-weather training. Why train in cold, wet Hampshire in January when you could be in sunny California? And so the pattern evolved of training in California during the early months of the year, returning to Britain in mid-May to embark on the European athletics season. In winter, he trained six days a week, a combination of road work, hill running, and about two track sessions per week, where the emphasis alternated between speed and hurdling technique.

Writing in the *Guardian* some years ago, Kriss made an interesting distinction between different periods of the year:

In winter I train, in the summer I practise – a subtle but important distinction. Three hours a day, six days a week. While the day is short and the light is short, I push my body to the limits. One more repetition...just a little faster. April 21, the spring equinox, the scales tip, the balance changes. Speed, technique and lots of rest.

The training routine in California was: get to the track at 10.00 or 11.00 a.m. and work until about 2.00 p.m. The rest of the day was spent with the family relaxing or, in later years, studying. With Daley Thompson, Roger Black and others, the training company was always good and it was a good place in which to be focused on the task.

> The main thing for me about going to America is that it's a place to relax. There's warm weather, obviously...More importantly, I can get away from the commercial aspects of track and field – TV and radio work, paper work, visiting schools, opening shops, telephone links, etc. Nobody knows me there. (Mel Watman interview in *Athletics Today*)

Throughout this period, Kriss had continued his spiritual journey. He read the Bible. He studied Josephus, the Jewish historian, and was amazed to discover that he wrote about this 'Jesus, whom some call the Christ'. Josephus did not believe in Jesus but he affirmed his existence as a historical figure. That helped Kriss in his investigation.

He read the letters of Pliny to the Emperor, seeking advice on how to deal with Christians in the

Roman Empire. It was becoming clearer that Jesus was not just a fairy-tale – not like Father Christmas and the tooth fairy. At this stage, Kriss's verdict was:

> Yes, there was a man called Jesus who walked on this earth. Many things convinced me of this including the fact that our dating system is based on Jesus – BC and AD. The references to Jesus in contemporary Jewish and Roman writings all convinced me that he had really lived on earth.

The writings of C. S. Lewis also helped Kriss. He was particularly challenged by a paragraph in *Mere Christianity*:

> I am trying here to prevent anyone here from saying the really foolish thing that people often say about [Jesus]: 'I'm ready to accept Jesus as a great moral teacher, but I don't accept His claim to be God.' This is the one thing we must not say. A man who was merely a man and said the sort of things Jesus said would not be a great moral teacher. He would either be a lunatic – on a level with the man who says he is a poached egg – or else he would be the Devil of Hell...You can shut Him up for a fool, you can spit at Him and kill Him as a demon; or you can fall at His feet and call Him Lord and God. But let us not come with any patronizing nonsense about His being a great human teacher. He has not left that open to us. He did not intend to.

After finding out about Jesus the historical figure, Kriss was still left feeling, 'OK – Great! – I would love to live by what you are saying but it is very, very hard.'

On 13 April 1987, Kriss was more or less still at this point. That night as he went to sleep, he prayed a prayer which went something like this: 'Well, Jesus, if you are who you say you are, how come I don't know you? If you are there, come and say "Hi" to Kriss.' He got more than he bargained for!

> That night I had a vision or a very vivid dream. I can remember that I was on the river bank and I heard some words being read out of a book. I remember feeling compelled to go towards the voice and I remember jumping in the water and swimming towards the voice. It was very hard going, like swimming uphill. Then all of a sudden the current changed and it started taking me faster than I wanted to go. I was getting really, really scared and all of a sudden I heard the words, 'Come to me, all you who are weary and burdened, and I will give you rest' (Matthew 11:28).
>
> As I heard these words, a great giant figure of Jesus came out of the water and I headed straight for the figure and shouted 'Jesus!' at the top of my voice.
>
> The problem was that I was sharing a room with Roger Black at the time and it's not cool to shout 'Jesus!' in the middle of the night! As I woke up, I remembered the dream and had a

real feeling of peace and tranquillity. Then I wrote down everything in a filofax that was lying by my bed. I went back to sleep and next morning when I woke up, the first thing I did was to look at the filofax and sure enough there was the account of my dream. It had really happened. In that moment all my 'head knowledge' about Jesus went into my heart. I was pumped up.

Later that morning I went down the track to train with Ed Moses, Roger Black, Daley Thompson, etc., and I told them, 'Hey guys, I saw Jesus last night!'

They all thought Kriss was crazy but he was serious, and he's been telling people ever since about meeting Jesus.

6

Over the Hurdles

Kriss had run his first 400 metres hurdles race back in 1983, clocking 55.0 in an early season meet. At the time, he had been struggling to break 48 seconds for the 400 metres flat, and someone had suggested that he try the hurdles. This is how he recalls this early experiment with hurdling:

> Well, I won the race but it was terrible. I ran and I stuttered, I ran and I stuttered. The funny thing is that the following week I ran the sprints in 10.7 and 21.6 – a massive improvement on my basic speed, and then at the UK Championships I ran 46.85 in second place and I thought to myself, 'Forget the hurdles!' I was on my way as a 400 metre runner.

In 1987, when he launched his second career at the age of 28, his approach to hurdling was altogether more serious. There was no such simple solution to his problems in making progress on the flat as there had been four years earlier.

In an interview at about this time in *21CC*, a Christian magazine, he referred to the Army as his job and running as his hobby. These priorities were to change pretty soon.

On 16 May, he took part in an international 400 metres hurdles race in Granada in Spain. It was his third hurdles race, discounting the one-off in 1983. In the first, he failed to finish. The second was a relatively low-level event which he won in 51.9. In Granada he came second in a time of 50.16, which *Athletics Today* recorded as a personal best – hardly surprising as it was his first serious attempt at the distance!

Two weeks later, he was first equal in the UK championships in 49.56. According to John Rodda in the *Guardian*, he 'plunged into his new career like a wallowing rhino and came home sharing the UK championship record with Max Robertson'. In June, he was selected to run for Britain against Czechoslovakia and Italy, coming second in 50.44.

Kriss's belief that he could become UK number one and make it into the British team was clearly vindicated by his progress in the first month of the 1987 season. His own assessment was:

I couldn't believe it when I ran 49.56 seconds to dead-heat with Max Robertson at the UK Championships, as in my first attempt over the hurdles at a little college meeting in America, I had fallen at the eighth barrier. Mind you, having already run 50.12 seconds in Granada, I realized I was going the right way. The moment I tied with Max Robertson at the UK Championships, I knew I had made the right decision. I may have looked untidy and people laughed at me, talking about my hop, skip and jump approach to winning races. But I was winning some and doing well where it mattered.

Kriss had four more significant races that summer in his build-up to the World Championships – if he was selected! He came fifth in the Peugeot Talbot games at Crystal Palace, third in Great Britain v. USA in Birmingham, and second in La Coruña. In the IAC meeting at Crystal Palace in mid-August, he came second in 49.34, another personal best.

He also entered the AAA championships in the 400 metres flat. His time of 46.13 and fifth place was further confirmation that his future lay over the hurdles not the flat.

One Sunday in the spring of 1987, Kriss decided to go to church and chose the Southampton Christian Fellowship. The minister, Paul Finn, recalls that he was 'just another visitor to the morning service. Granted, he looked fitter than most and his broad smile made him very endearing.' Over the next 10 years, Paul was to see a great deal more of Kriss as he settled into the church which, in turn, has sought to treat him as far as possible like a normal member, although, admittedly, not many other members have a laugh like his! It was the start of a valuable relationship with the church, where he is still a member.

He was duly selected for the World Championships in Rome in 1987 in the 400 metres hurdles. The experience of competing in a major championship was not new to Kriss but the event was. He was certainly glad to be there.

So swift had been his progress in the hurdles, that here he was, one year after switching events, already in the World Championships. He was on form for the event. In the first heat he ran 49.36, only two hundredths of a second outside his personal best. He came second in the heat. In the semi-final he came third, but it had required another personal best, 48.64, to do so.

He came seventh in the final in 48.74, which, until the previous day, would have been a personal best. Ed Moses won the race from Danny Harris, beating Kriss by about 10 metres.

To come from winning in Reading in 51.9 seconds to finishing seventh in the world in 48.74 in the space of four months, and to make the final of the World Championships less than a year after deciding to take up the event was a fairy-tale achievement. The icing on the cake was a silver medal in the relay, with Kriss running the second leg in 44.60 as Britain set a new British and European record of 2:58.86.

One thing which was different about Rome – apart from the change of event – was Kriss's attitude.

I was very conscious of God's presence with me in Rome. I went to the athletes' Christian fellowship meeting. I prayed before my races – not that I would win but that God would bring out the best in me. On the blocks I am usually very nervous but this time I felt very calm.

His winter work was delayed by a hernia operation, in the autumn. This was to rectify damage caused, in all probability, by pushing himself too hard on the circuits – a strategy devised to develop his strength and stamina for the hurdles.

The task in the winter was to continue developing and honing the hurdling technique. The goal was the European Championships in 1990 but the best possible achievement in the 1988 Olympics was also not to be sneezed at.

1987 had been a year of change. As well as a new event, Kriss gained a new daughter, Shakira. The following year brought with it a further significant milestone in his life. In early 1988 when Kriss was in California the church he was going to, Calvary Chapel, announced that there would be a baptism service. The invitation was for all those who were Christians and who wanted to take the opportunity to make a public witness to their faith to be baptized. Kriss had been a Christian for one year and decided that the time was right for him to be baptized.

One Saturday morning on a California beach, he was baptized in the Pacific Ocean with hundreds of people there. Kriss recalls 'going into the sea which was lovely and warm, being baptized and coming out and giving high fives to everyone, as a "Welcome to the Kingdom!"'

1988 proved to be a year of consolidation rather than progress. His best early season performance was a win in Helsinki in 49.10. In August, he had three runs in ten days on the Grand Prix circuit. In Zurich he came fourth in 48.67, just three hundredths of a second outside his personal best. In Cologne, he was second in 48.89 and fifth in the Grand Prix final in Berlin in a disappointing 50.57.

There was one supreme irony in the 1988 season. Remember that Kriss had changed events in 1986 because he did not feel confident that he would ever again be selected for a major championship in the 400 metres flat. Before the 1988 Olympics, the selectors announced that the AAA championship would be a kind of Olympic trial. Anyone who finished first in an event, and who had achieved the Olympic qualifying standard, would gain automatic selection to the Games. Other places would be at the discretion of the selectors.

As UK number one in the hurdles, Kriss was entirely confident of selection for the Olympics. He felt that, with due respect to his fellow competitors, he was unlikely to be pushed in the 400 metres hurdles. He felt that a fast race on the flat could be more beneficial to his preparations for Seoul. He entered the 400 metres flat with this in mind. To his surprise he won the race in a personal best time of 44.93. His previous best of 45.43, set in the 1984 Olympics, had stood for four years.

His own reaction was:

That gave me immense pleasure! All of a sudden here I was, now a 400m hurdler but still with a lot of passion for the flat, finally achieving my great ambition of breaking 45 seconds. I'm satisfied. I don't need to run another 400, and probably won't. (Mel Watman interview in *Athletics Today*)

Kriss was quick to announce that the race had been a training exercise and that he wished to run the hurdles in Seoul. He did not wish to take up his automatic 400 metres flat place in the team.

In the four years since the Los Angeles Olympics, a great deal had happened in Kriss's life. He had switched events to the 400 metres hurdles. He had also become a Christian. 1988 was a lot more serious for Kriss than the previous Olympics. In 1984, he had gone to enjoy himself and to do the best he could. By 1988, he had sufficient credibility in athletics to expect to make the final, and possibly actually achieve one of the first three places.

In the event, despite a slight injury problem, he made the final – but only just – coming fourth in his semi-final with four reaching the final. In a TV interview, he said of his injury, 'I'll be OK so long as all the Christians out there keep praying.' In the final, he came sixth in a time of 48.69. It was probably all that he could have expected at that stage of his development as a hurdler. His time was almost identical to the one he had run in Rome in the World Championship the previous year – 48.69 to 48.74, and only five hundredths of a second off his personal best.

He had the satisfaction too of being the first European to finish. The race was won by André Phillips, with the legendary Ed Moses third – Moses's second defeat in eleven years. Afterwards, André Phillips said, 'I watched Edwin Moses in the 1976 Olympics in Montreal and I've been chasing him ever since.' When Kriss was once asked if he had ever run with Ed Moses, he replied, quick as a flash, 'No, I can't say I have. I've been in the same races as him. I've run behind him but I can't say that I've run with him!'

Fourth and fifth places in that Olympic final went to Kevin Young and Winthrop Graham, two men who would cross Kriss's path a few more times before the story was concluded.

The 1988 Olympic 4 × 400 relay saw a reasonable performance but no medal for Britain. The team finished fifth in 3 minutes 2 seconds dead, nearly three seconds slower than in 1984. *Athletics Today* reported: 'Any chance of a medal was lost when anchorman Phil Brown was obstructed as he set off. The loss of Derek Redmond through injury proved too great a blow, even though Brian Whittle, Kriss Akabusi, Todd Bennett and Phil Brown ran their hearts out.' Kriss ran the second leg in 44.73.

The 1988 Olympics represented a very significant stage in the development of Christian ministry to sports events. 1988 saw British chaplains to the Olympics for the first time. In 1984, there was scarcely a committed Christian in the British team. In 1988, there was a growing Christian presence. As well as Kriss, there was the long jumper/sprinter, Barrington

Williams, triple jumpers Vernon Samuels and Jonathan Edwards, and the 400 metres runner Loreen Hall.

Loreen Hall made quite an impact on her room-mate, Judy Simpson (alias Gladiator Nightshade), in what was otherwise a disastrous Olympics for Judy. This is how Judy recalls the 1988 Olympics:

In athletics terms I had the worst major competition I ever had in my life. The heptathlon is a seven-event competition and in the second event of the seven, I was injured and had to retire from my third Olympic Games. It was a disaster. But I didn't have a bad Olympics when I think about it because I met some fantastic people. I was sharing a room with Loreen Hall, a very gifted and talented 400 metres runner. She had a regime that I was very impressed with. She used to wake up and pray and think about how she was going to spend her day, how she was going to be as positive as she could about it.

Sharing a room with someone like that who had such a belief and whose faith was rock-solid helped me to see again that Jesus was someone who had to be in my life to help me lead a better life, a fuller life. And then I met some fantastic people – Kriss Akabusi and Jonathan Edwards and people like that, and the way they lived their life really impressed me. That introduced me again to the Christian faith.

Jonathan Edwards has said of this period:

> We had a lot of meetings together. There was a
> kind of spontaneity. It was the start of the Chris-
> tians in Sport in athletics movement. We all felt
> that we were at the beginning of something that
> was quite important.

The Christian athletes had in fact started meeting
together in Japan, where they had been for a training
camp just prior to Seoul. Peter Swaffield, one of the
Olympic chaplains, recalls inviting Kriss and other
British athletes to the chapel services which were
planned for each day.

Kriss replied, 'Certainly we want to meet every day,
but let's do it out in the open so that everyone can join
us as they want, not hidden away in chapel somewhere.'
Such an initiative by the chaplains would have been
frowned upon by the Games Committee, but as it was
the athletes' idea – no problem. The meeting took place
every evening at 6.00 p.m., in the open air in the Plaza.

A particularly memorable meeting was held on the
night before the 4 × 400 metres relay final, with three
of the finalists represented – Kriss Akabusi from UK,
Innocent Egbunike of Nigeria, and America's Danny
Everett.

As each one prayed, Egbunike's prayer was 'Lord, I
don't ask that I should win tomorrow, but please,
please don't let me finish behind Akabusi.' The meeting ended in chaotic laughter. (For the record, Nigeria
were seventh to Britain's fifth.)

One incident during those Olympics illustrated Kriss's growing fervour for his Christian faith. Two athletes who were not Christians came to the athletes' Bible study. Everyone was having a great time singing. These two girls enjoyed the singing. During the Bible study the girls said, 'There are many ways to God and if you say that God loves us he's not going to be bad to us, is he?' Kriss stood up and said, 'The Bible says that Jesus is the way, the truth and life. No one can come to the Father except through him. If you don't accept him you are going to hell.'

Some of the others were surprised at Kriss's forthright response. He too wondered if he had come across 'too heavy', but in the end he felt he had been right not to compromise the truth.

Kriss's own end-of-term report on the 1988 season was, 'I confirmed myself by being the first European to finish at the Olympic Games running 48.69 seconds in sixth position.'

However, his progress in times had been a little disappointing. In the *Athletics Today* interview, Mel Watman asked him, 'In your first season [1987] you ran 48.64, which was a tremendous start, but in the following two seasons you virtually stagnated with best times of 48.67 in 1988 and 48.59 in 1989. This was somewhat reminiscent of the time you were stuck at 48 seconds for the flat 400. Did you ever feel that this was as fast as you would get?'

Kriss replied: 'You always wonder, but I was hoping that history would just repeat itself – that eventually the times would drop. Like when I ran 48 seconds so

many times, and when I improved from running so
often around 45.5 to 44.93 in 1988. After running
about 48.6 for the hurdles so many times I thought it
just couldn't be my absolute personal best.'

There was no rest following the Olympics but
instead a long winter, which started in September
1988, to prepare for the rigours of the Commonwealth
Games fourteen months later, followed by the European Championships that summer.

By now, Kriss's Christian faith was growing and domi-
nating more of his life, including track and field. Well-
meaning Christian folk sometimes asked him if
athletics was an appropriate job for a Christian. Athletics coaches and administrators wondered if the
'born-again Akabusi' would be as competitive as previously. Kriss, with the help of Christian friends, worked
through these questions and came to this conclusion:

> Before I was Christian, track and field was very
> important to me because it was a way of my say-
> ing 'I'm your equal'. I was brought up in a chil-
> dren's home and I was always struggling to say
> 'I am as good as you – don't patronize me'. In
> becoming a Christian, I no longer feel the need
> to declare that I know I am your equal.
>
> As far as competitiveness is concerned, I was
> competitive before I was a Christian and I am
> extra competitive now that I am a Christian. I
> realized that my ability had been given to me by
> God and there is a verse in the Bible which says

that we are not to bury our talents. I believe God has given me this gift so that I can express his glory within myself but also so that I can touch other people's lives. As a Christian I still want to win, but not at all costs and if I cross the line second, third or worse I don't have to kick the timing machine or look at someone else and feel angry with him. That is a small indication of what God has done for me over the past few years.

Roger Black and Kriss started a business together in 1988. It was about health and fitness, stress relief and a healthy lifestyle. It was aimed at communicating to business people that if they gave some thought to the health and fitness of their employees they would benefit by getting better productivity, fewer days off sick and so on. The approach was very big in America and they had the idea of promoting it in the UK. They set up a company with two businessmen. They were looking at the business as their future. However, one of the businessmen was always looking for a quick profit and Roger and Kriss were not happy with that approach so they wound up the business within one year.

1989 was potentially a quiet year. There were no major championships that year, although the Europa Cup – a team competition between the countries of Europe – was in Gateshead and Britain was, therefore, keener than ever to do well.

For Kriss, however, it was a vital season. He was half-way through his four-year plan which was supposed to culminate in the gold medal in the European

Championships in 1990. He had had a great start in 1987, had consolidated in 1988 but needed, in 1989, to make a further stride forward.

What complicated 1989 was that there was only a short winter. Normally, athletes finish their season in September, have a break, restart training, possibly have a quick flutter on the indoor season before beginning again in earnest in May of the following year.

The problem with that schedule was that the 1990 Commonwealth Games in Auckland were in January, when, in normal years, Kriss would have been in training in California. The 1989 season, therefore, had to take account of the requirements of 1990.

Kriss had four early season races in Modesto, Columbus, Granada and Seville, getting progressively quicker, culminating in 49.04 in Seville.

He ran for Britain in Birmingham against USA, USSR and West Germany on 23 June. The night before, Kriss was at a packed Crystal Palace. Nothing unusual about that, but on this occasion he wasn't running. It was part of Billy Graham's Mission to London and Kriss was speaking. This is part of what he said:

> When I was young, like most people I wanted to know the meaning of life. Why was I here? Where was I going? I decided that the aim of life was to get as much as I could for myself...
>
> By and large I succeeded. In 1984 I won an Olympic silver medal. With that came some sort of fame and fortune – I'm not Rockefeller but most things I want I can have. I have a nice

house. I always wanted to have a Mercedes and now I have two. So everything I really wanted, I got.

The funny thing was that none of these things ever fully satisfied me. No sooner had I got something than there was something else I wanted. I began to say 'there has to be another meaning to life'.

Then I heard about Jesus. Of course, I'd heard about him before but I never realized that he walked on earth and that he had said so many amazing things like the verse on the scoreboard over there, 'I am the way, the truth and the life' [John 14:6], or 'I am come that you might have life and have it abundantly' [John 10:10]. Jesus promised eternal life to anyone who believes in him.

When I realized all these things about Jesus I just knew that I had a decision to make. I started investigating to find out if it was really true what he said. Two years ago I made a decision to give my life to Jesus Christ. I just thank the Lord for all that he has done for me.

I want to say to anyone who is not a Christian that you are faced with the biggest decision of your life. I just pray that you will open your eyes and ears and that Christ will bless us with his gift of eternal life. Guys, I tell you, I had a good time before I was Christian but I've had a better time since.

There were over twenty thousand people present at Crystal Palace but that was only a fraction of the number who listened to Kriss that night. The meeting was broadcast live by satellite link to locations all over the UK, as well as to several African countries.

The Europa Cup was scheduled for Friday 5 and Saturday 6 August in Gateshead. Eight countries compete in twenty events, one competitor per country per event, with the winning team the one which gains most points over the twenty events – eight for first place, seven for second, etc. There is a parallel women's event alongside the men's.

The event is traditionally dominated by the Russians and the East Germans. This year there was no reason why it should have been different, but the British were determined to give it a go.

The first event was the 400 metres hurdles, with Harald Schmidt of Germany in the field. Kriss was not in the best of shape. He had been injured for four weeks and only had ten days' training behind him. He was so concerned that he might let the team down that he came close to dropping out. In an exchange with team manager, Frank Dick, just before the race, Kriss remarked, 'Things don't get any easier.' Dick retorted, 'That's what makes champions out of people.'

Kriss went out and ran 48.95 to win the race from Harald Schmidt (49.26) to give Britain the perfect start. It was without doubt his best performance so far in the hurdles. It was a great victory. This is Kriss's own account of the race, as recorded in *Athletics Weekly*:

I told myself I was going to have to dig very deep. I was also worried that even if my leg held up I might die a death in the last 100. I was worried about totally falling apart.

I got into the blocks and normally I then lose those sort of nerves. But I was still fighting myself. There was a false start and I just stayed in my blocks. I got up, turned to the crowd and sort of put my arms out and shrugged my shoulders, as if saying, 'What can you do?' and I smiled. They all laughed and that eased my tension. Then I thought, 'Go and do the business!' I thought Harald Schmidt would win it but I didn't want to lose to the young Czech who had run 48.9.

When I went to the blocks for the second time, I said a little prayer. I had calmed down a bit and went out very controlled. I found myself up there alongside Schmidt. The crowd was cheering, there was a realization I was up there at the front, the adrenaline was flowing and there was also the realization that I could get more points than I had been tipped to get. That was all going through my mind as I took hurdle nine. At hurdle ten I thought, 'Don't fall over and make a fool of yourself.' I felt relief to reach the line first, and very happy.

This was probably the first time – but very far from the last – that Kriss had been a real inspiration to the whole team. Boy, did they respond! Linford Christie in the 100 metres, John Regis in the 200 metres, Tom McKean in the 800 metres, Colin Jackson in the 100 metres hurdles, Dalton Grant in the high jump and Steve Backley in the javelin were also winners for Britain. The 4 × 100 metres relay team pulled it off, too.

With Britain in the lead overall, the final event was the 4 × 400 relay. Provided they avoided a disaster and finished ahead of the Russians, Britain would win the Europa Cup. If ever there was a time for a cautious run it was now. However, the word 'cautious' was not in their vocabulary. The team of Peter Crampton, Kriss, Todd Bennett and Brian Whittle, running in that order, went out and won the race in 3:03.16, with the West Germans just behind in 3:03.33.

On the first leg, Peter Crampton edged ahead of the Russian. Kriss made more progress on the second leg and put the team in fourth place. Todd Bennett finished his leg in third place. Then, on the final leg, Brian Whittle came storming home.

For the first time, Britain had won the Europa Cup and had qualified for the World Cup final. The women's team had a creditable performance too, coming third in their match behind the East Germans and Russians.

The *Daily Mail* reported the victory on page one under a headline 'Tomorrow the World', describing it as 'Britain's athletes' finest hour, defeating the once-invincible Russians and East Germans to be crowned track and field kings of Europe'.

7

Going for Gold

The win in the 1989 Europa Cup had been a great confidence booster. It confirmed Kriss as European number one. It was not a coincidental happening, it was all part of the plan. As Kriss said: 'This was the beginning of my purple patch and I will not kid you – it was planned to take me to the winner's rostrum in Split.'

Reaching the World Championship final in 1987 and the Olympic final in 1988 had been good. However, 1990 had always been the year that Kriss and Mike Whittingham had been aiming at. For a man who had never hurdled to be planning within four years to win gold medals at Commonwealth and European Championships – and, what's more, to have a jolly good go at the British record which had stood since David Hemery's Olympic gold medal at altitude in Mexico in 1968 – was on the face of it presumptuous.

Yet, when 1990 dawned, Kriss and his coach knew that they had done the groundwork and were ready for the onslaught on 1990. With the Commonwealth Games in Auckland in mid-January, Kriss was already having a warm-up race in Sydney on 14 January. He won in a time of 49.96. A week later and he was winning again in 49.03, less than half a second outside his personal best.

When the Commonwealth Games started he won his heat in 49.86, and the following day took the gold in 48.89. He had been the clear favourite to win but he was not so confident himself, recognizing that it was by far the biggest race he had so far encountered. (It was bigger than the Olympic final in the sense that he was here to win – not something that he had had realistic hopes of in the 1988 Olympics.)

He told *Athletics Weekly*, 'The race went as planned but I know I can run faster. I'll have to wait until the summer to meet the big boys.' *Athletics Weekly* also quoted him as saying, 'I didn't get Alan Pascoe's 1974 record but I did the next best thing,' and also commented that Kriss 'followed his win with a far more successful attempt at hurdling the wrong way over the last flight of hurdles than Pascoe did at Christchurch sixteen years ago when he set a Games record of 48.83 to lift gold.' Pascoe had followed his success by falling over the hurdle!

Receiving the gold medal for England was a very special moment, as Kriss recalled:

For a sportsman to stand on the rostrum and be recognized by everyone for his achievement is a very important occasion. The privilege of being in the number one position and seeing the flag of your country go up, and hearing the national anthem, perhaps catching a glimpse of yourself on the big screen, perhaps a re-run of your race – you get a lump in your throat and think 'My word!' People elevate you but I know who I am and therefore for me to see myself on the big screen, see the flag, hear the national anthem and realize that over ninety thousand people in the stadium are sharing that moment, it is actually a real humbling experience.

England were hot favourites for the 4 × 400 metres relay gold medal. However, they were denied the chance by the controversial disqualification of the team over a baton change. In fact, England, Australia, and Trinidad and Tobago were all disqualified.

With a first hurdling gold medal under his belt, Kriss set off for California to focus on his preparations for the 1990 European summer season and ultimately the European Championships.

He did not run a bad race all summer. He won in Granada in 48.70. That was his first major race of the summer and already he was a fifth of a second faster than in the Commonwealth gold medal race. Less than a week after Granada he was coming fourth in Seville – equalling his personal best of 48.59 to do so. In June, he won the UK Championships in Cardiff and came first in two internationals – GB v. USA and Kenya in Portsmouth, and GB v. German Democratic Republic and Canada in Gateshead.

In July and August, he continued to run races around the world, including the European Grand Prix circuit. He was fourth in La Coruña – again under 49 seconds; second in New York, second in Malmo, first in Lahti and first in Monte Carlo.

On 15 August he was fourth in Zürich, but ran a personal best of 48.34. He was in just the kind of shape he wanted to be in when he set off for Split in what was then Yugoslavia.

In his heat, Kriss ran 50.08, but that was good enough not only to win the heat comfortably but also to be the fastest qualifier. He won his semi-final in 48.84, with the Swede, Niklas Wallenlind, being marginally faster in the other semi-final.

For the final, Kriss's race plan was based on a belief that no one else in the field could run faster than 48.8. He was confident that he could run 48.4, which should be enough for a comfortable victory. He set off steadily, but was disturbed to see Sven Nylander of Sweden still in contention at the fifth hurdle. He made his move, saying, as he likes to tell it, 'See ya' to Nylander as he set off for the finish. He won by half a second or four metres from Nylander, with Wallenlind third.

Athletics Weekly reported the race like this:

Akabusi made a controlled, almost cautious start to the final – 'I wanted to clear the first five hurdles cleanly without any mistakes in thirteen strides and I did just that'. [Hurdling is a very technical event with runners varying the number of strides they take between hurdles according to their level of fitness, the speed of the race, etc.] From then on the plan formulated with coach Mike Whittingham was to run thirteen

strides to hurdle seven, fourteen to nine and fif-
teen home. 'That was deliberately playing it
safe,' said Whittingham, 'and Kriss reckoned it
cost him 0.3 second by changing down.'

So Kriss had won his gold medal and that was that.
Well, not quite. Kriss was so happy with his victory
that he was celebrating with anyone and everyone. He
spoke to a group of British supporters. Someone said,
'Kriss, look at the scoreboard!' He carried on talking
and enjoying his triumph. They said again, 'Kriss, look
at the scoreboard!'

He looked round and saw: KRISS AKABUSI 47.92,
NEW BRITISH RECORD. As Cheryl Baker once said,
'When this guy reacts, boy! does he react!' Kriss started pointing at the scoreboard with a look of amaze-
ment. He started running around – even faster than
he'd run in the race! Eventually, he dropped to his
knees for a prayer of 'Thank you, Lord.'

John Rodda in the *Guardian* made a good attempt
to describe the scene he witnessed:

He suddenly went berserk, scuttling on the track
like a rabbit found by a fox. He pranced, leapt,
punched the air, knelt and prayed. It was a win
for Christians in Sport, a win for the Army and a
win for Mike Whittingham.

His time of 47.92 was a British record. He was the first
Briton ever under 48 seconds. He was the ninth
fastest of all time. He had every right to celebrate.

Kriss had had a weekly reminder of David Hemery's pre-eminence. He did most of his hurdling training at Broadbridge Heath in Horsham. On the wall, there is a mural of David Hemery in action with Kriss just behind him. Some wag suggested that the local council should redo the mural to put Akabusi ahead of Hemery!

After the dust had settled, Kriss told *Athletics Weekly* what it all meant to him:

I must admit that my victory in Split was the most emotional moment of my athletics career. I know I went loopy but there was a relief at having won, which was expected, as that was my whole intention of going to the championships. However, I can now tell you that on the way to the stadium I told Roger Black, 'I'm going to run 47.95 today.'

It was almost half a minute after the finish that I saw my time and I thought someone was stitching me up, it had to be a joke. However, when the full realization what I had run hit me, all I wanted to do was rush around and tell somebody and then it was after this loopy period that I settled down and said 'Thank you Lord'.

I am part of history. I am the European Champion. I'm the number one hurdler in Europe. I know for some people it is old hat but for me it's obviously a source of pride. It's unbelievable. Not only did I break David Hemery's record but I'm the first Briton to run under 48 seconds. That's why I was so crazy – because I made history.

Athletics Today described the 4 × 400 metres relay as a 'superb end to a superb championship'. It was Britain's ninth gold medal, which, along with their five silver and four bronze, made for an amazing haul.

The relay was remarkable in itself for the presence of John Regis who had, just an hour and forty minutes earlier, been in the British 4 × 100 relay team which came second – to add to his 100 metre bronze and 200 metres gold.

Britain came second in their heat, behind Italy, with Kriss running the second leg in an otherwise almost reserve team. In the final, they ran 2:58.22 for a new European record to finish over two seconds ahead of the German Federal Republic. Paul Sanders ran the first leg in 45.85, Kriss's second leg was 44.48. He handed over to John Regis before Roger Black ran 43.96 to lead Britain home.

Another encouragement from Split was Mark McAllister from Christians in Sport, who led nine Bible studies for the athletes in the course of the week of the championships.

1990 had been the year on which Kriss had set his sights when he took the decision in the winter of 1986 to switch to the hurdles. He had finished the year as Commonwealth and European champion and had broken David Hemery's 22-year-old British record for good measure. In his spare time, he had picked up a gold medal in the relay in a European record time.

His end-of-term report was very satisfactory, yet he had a sneaking feeling that he could still do better.

8

The Mother of All Relay Races

The 1991 athletics season is best remembered for what Saddam Hussein might have called the mother of all relay races. The 4 × 400 metres for men in the World Championship final certainly was one of the most exciting races of all time. However, that race came at the end of a long 1991 season. For Kriss, there were a lot of hurdles to clear before he got there.

It was a good season for Kriss, starting with second place in the 400 metres flat in the UK Championships in Cardiff. He won 400 metres hurdles races in Belfast, Crystal Palace, Sheffield, Gateshead and Edinburgh. There was also first place in the Europa Cup in Frankfurt in 48.39.

Before one event in Stockholm, Jonathan Edwards found Kriss a less than ideal room-mate:

Kriss snores extremely loudly, and half way through the night with a competition the next day I decided this was enough. I had to sleep. Fortunately there were two rooms in this hotel apartment. I slept on a couch and next morning

Kriss woke up and thought, 'Where's Jonathan?' He came through, burst out in that laugh that only Kriss can produce and said, 'Oh no, my snoring's kept you awake!' But he is a lot of fun and good to share with. I just take ear plugs now if I'm sharing.

On hearing Jonathan tell this story Kriss, quick as a flash, claimed a share in Jonathan's world record. How come? 'Well, just think how far he has been jumping since he stopped sharing with me!'

Thirty-five runners were included in the field for the 400 metres hurdles in the 1991 World Championships in Tokyo. There were five heats then the semi-finals and the final between the runners and a medal.

At the beginning of the season Kriss's assessment of his prospects was:

I think I have a possibility of winning the World Championships but there is more chance of me not winning. If I come first, second, third – great! But, being realistic, I'm just as likely to come fifth. If I were to run 47.7 or 47.8 for fifth I would personally be disappointed but it would be no disgrace.

Kriss won his heat in 48.79, one of only three runners to go under 49 seconds. He also won his semi-final in 47.91, breaking his own British and European record by one hundredth of a second. He was the only athlete under 48 seconds so far. His reaction to his second

British record was in stark contrast to his first. At Split, in the European Championships, he had run around the track and gone 'loopy'. This time – admittedly it was just a heat – he strolled quietly from the track.

By the fourth day of the World Championships, Britain had not yet picked up a medal. Colin Jackson, hot favourite for the 110 metres hurdles, withdrew with injury. Linford Christie and John Regis were eliminated in the heats of the 200 metres. Tom McKean, Steve Backley and Yvonne Murray brought the number of British European Champions who failed to win a medal in the World Championships to six.

However, that fourth day of the championships, 27 August, was the day of the 400 metres hurdles final. Kriss was there as European Champion and certainly was in form, as his new UK record in the semi-final showed. His record was to last but 48 hours, as he broke it again in the final.

The result of the 1991 World Championships 400 metres hurdles final was:

1st	Samuel Matete	47.64
2nd	Winthrop Graham	47.74
3rd	Kriss Akabusi	47.86
4th	Kevin Young	48.01
5th	Danny Harris	48.46

Kriss had taken the bronze medal, broken his own British and European record and finished ahead of the World number one, Danny Harris. He must be pleased with that, surely? But Kriss rang Monika shortly after the race and told her he'd blown it. He felt the race was there for the winning and he'd failed.

At the half-way stage, Kriss was fifth but ran a good bend to close on Young and Harris. As they approached the final hurdle Kriss was in third place but still closing fast on the two leaders, running – as *Athletics Today* put it – 'like the Tokyo Bullet train'! Then, in his own words, 'I made a basic mistake. I lost concentration and thought about what the others were doing instead of what I was doing. I hit the final hurdle and struggled from then on. I was relaxed as I came over the ninth hurdle and I thought I could take Winthrop and possibly Samuel. Then I took my mind off hurdling, thinking about those two ahead.'

It certainly looked as if he would have taken silver and even pressed Samuel Matete hard for the gold, had he not hit the hurdle. At the beginning of the championships Kriss would probably have settled for a bronze. In the event, he realized that without that small error of judgement the colour of his medal could been different. After all it was only 0.24 of a second between Kriss's third place and the gold medal.

Tokyo represented another step forward for the Christian group in British athletics as they met regularly for Bible study, considering the practical implications of the Christian life through a study of 1 Corinthians. The chaplain, Mark McAllister, wrote of the week, 'If the theme of our meetings could be encapsulated in a single phrase, it would be our desire to build with "gold, silver and precious stones" (1 Corinthians 3:12).

We believe that God wants a continuing Christian presence in the team and all the Christian athletes to grow to maturity. It is hard not to get excited about what God is doing in British athletics.'

It is hard to think of running a personal best, breaking the British and European record and winning a World Championship medal being eclipsed within a week. But that is exactly what happened. The 4 × 400 metres relay for men became the race of the championships.

Britain had been a force to reckon with in the 4 x 400 metres for almost a decade. The success can be attributed partly to having a good squad of runners at 400 metres and partly to the ability to produce the goods on the day, to run out of their skins and so to beat runners who on paper were superior.

Britain's track record in the 4 × 400 relay in the period coming up to the 1991 World Championships was good:

1983	World Championships	Bronze
1984	Olympics	Silver
1986	European Championships	Gold
	Commonwealth Games (as England)	Gold
1987	World Championships	Silver
1988	Olympics	Fifth
1990	European Championships	Gold

As Peter Nichols wrote in the *Observer*, the team has had more shared wins than Torville and Dean.

This record bred confidence in the British camp, but the realists still had to see the Americans as the firm favourites. Kriss incidentally was quoted in an interview a year before, predicting, 'I reckon we could run 2:56 and beat any American team. Men of the calibre of Danny Everett and Steve Lewis are great guys but I think we can beat them.'

Britain won their heat in 2:59.49, breaking the three-minute barrier, which was now becoming routine. The team for the heat was Ade Mafe, Derek Redmond, Mark Richardson and Kriss, running the anchor leg.

When the final came, the strongest team was picked, with Roger Black and John Regis coming in for Mafe and Richardson. Britain took the initiative in the final by switching the expected order of the runners. Roger Black, the normal anchor man, would run first. John Regis was brought in to the team in the hope that his speed as a 200 metre specialist would be a real asset, provided his strength could carry him the extra distance.

The surprise to end all surprises was that 'Grandfather' Akabusi was to run the final leg. The original plan had been for John Regis to run the last leg, but, as he explained later, Kriss was very keen to take on that responsibility himself.

The race, the 43rd and last event of the World Championships, began with Roger Black, silver medallist in the individual 400 metres, facing the American Andrew Valmon. If the plan was to have any chance, Roger Black had to be ahead – and well ahead – at the first change-over. Black ran 44.7 to the American's 44.9. A good start, a lead of two metres but perhaps we had hoped for more. Quincey Watts produced one of the fastest ever relay legs – 43.4 to Redmond's 44.0. (The first leg is always slower than the later ones as it is from a standing start.) The Americans had a four-metre lead.

John Regis regained some of the lost ground with 44.22 against Danny Everett's 44.31. All the same, the World individual 400 metres Champion, Antonio Pettigrew still had a lead of between two and three metres on Kriss Akabusi.

Kriss used all his experience, gradually pegging the American back. By 200 metres he was on Pettigrew's shoulder. He stayed on his shoulder, attacking him on the final straight, passing him and just managing to stay ahead.

David Powell wrote in *The Times* of the final few seconds of the 1991 World Championships: 'There can have been few finer moments in British athletics. Stretching and straining every muscle, Akabusi dipped past Antonio Pettigrew of the United States in the last stride or two. As the finishing line drew closer, Akabusi's shoulders, arms, neck and torso overhung his tired legs and he inched the verdict.'

Kriss had run 44.59 to the American's 44.93. Britain had won in 2:57.53, a new European and Commonwealth record, beating the Americans by four hundredths of a second. In describing Kriss's tactics in that final leg, one could do worse than to recall the words of Eric Liddell on winning the gold medal at the 1924 Paris Olympics: 'I ran as fast as I could for the first half of the race and even faster in the second half.'

That this was the first British triumph over the Americans in the 4 × 400 metres since 1936, and the fact that the British time was the fourth fastest of all time – the Americans were fifth in the all-time list – is a further indication of the magnitude of the achievement.

Kriss's own account of the race, which he has retold hundreds of times, goes something like this:

Probably the most exciting race that I ever took part in was the 4 × 400 metres relay final in the World Championships in Tokyo in 1991. The British team had gone to Tokyo with high hopes but things didn't go according to plan. Several of our gold medal hopes either got injured or couldn't find their form. By the time the 4 × 400 metres relay came on the last day we just had three medals, one gold, a silver and my bronze in the 400 metres hurdles.

The Americans were the firm favourites in the relay but the British team just felt that perhaps we could do something that day. The Americans weren't impressed with our optimism. Their reaction was to dismiss us with a 'Gee, man, they're not worth bothering about. We're gonna kick their butts.'

We had come up with an unusual tactic for the race. We felt that we had to stay in touch with the Americans from the start. While it is usual in a relay to put your best man out last, we decided to put our fastest man, Roger Black, out in the first leg. That left us with another problem: who would run the last leg?

Well, the night before the race I went to bed thinking and praying. I was sharing a room with Roger Black. Suddenly this conversation took place.

Kriss:	Roger, I can do it!
Roger:	Kriss, you can do what?
Kriss:	I can run that last leg!
Roger:	Are you sure?
Kriss:	Yeah, yeah, yeah!

We went down to the manager and he said OK. 'Kriss wants to run last leg.'

'Are you sure Kriss?'

'Yes, I'm sure.'

The gun goes off and the race is on. Roger Black, our best man, sets off on the first leg. Remember – this is all-important. Roger needs to be right up there with the Americans to give us a chance. He is dependable, runs a great leg and puts us first. Next to go – Captain Courageous, Derek Redmond. Derek was the previous British record holder prior to Roger Black. Yet over the ensuing years he has had injury following injury. He had only trained three weeks prior to coming fourth in the European Championships in 1990.

This year we're in luck, he's in training six weeks and runs the second leg for us. He grabs the baton and runs great. He hands over the baton, level pegging with the Americans. Next to go Johnnie 'Two-chest' Regis, European Champion for 200 metres and 14.5 stone of pure British beef charging down the track, level pegging with the Americans, nostrils flaring, eyeballs popping, you get the picture – he means business! He's done his job and it's over to the old man.

I get the baton and I'm off. I charge round the bend after Pettigrew and all of a sudden I come off Pettigrew's shoulder. I'm thinking, 'Stay there, stay there...' All I see before me is a little bald head. All of a sudden I'm feeling 'Wow this thing's easy, yeah'. So, round that bend and coming to the home straight, I see this home straight and I think, 'OK this is it!' and I start flying past him, yeah! Oh man! And all of a sudden I'm getting about ten metres from the line and all of a sudden I feel him breathing down my neck and I think, 'Oh no, please God help me now so I cross that line.' And I'm so relieved! Fantastic, we crossed the line first. We'd won! What a terrific feeling!

When Kriss speaks about his life at business conferences, at schools, etc., the story of the Tokyo relay is retold, nay, acted out. Kriss always seems to tell it as if it is the first time he has ever recited it. Audiences, even though they know the outcome, are on the edge of their seats wondering if Akabusi will manage, on this occasion, to catch the American!

When he returned home, Kriss was amazed at the impact the race had had. Amused, in a mischievous way, at all those Christians who had struggled to watch the race – at 10.15 on Sunday morning – and still be at the 10.30 service! He commented: 'It's very funny, when you're out there doing your stuff you don't realize what effect you're having on the people back here. And when you came back to England you realize a lot of people follow you.'

Athletics is an individual sport. When the gun goes, you are on your own. It is an athlete's achievements in individual events which impress the sponsors and attract the big money. Nonetheless the members of the British 4 × 400 relay team that 1 September 1991 admit that they have never experienced a moment of such excitement as that relay victory. They had plotted a victory, out-strategized the Americans, and then had the ability and character to deliver when it mattered.

Michael Calvin, writing in the *Daily Telegraph*, gave much of the credit for the relay victory to Kriss – not just for a brilliant last leg but for his role within the team. He describes Kriss as 'the most popular athlete in the British squad. He has been the focal point of British effort in Japan, lifting morale at a critical time by winning Britain's first medal of the championships.'

As *The Times* said, 'Who would have thought that Kriss Akabusi could outsmile the smile he had given on winning the individual bronze medal!' The Akabusi smile was a great high on which to end the 1991 World Championships.

The team did one more event that year, not at Gateshead or Crystal Palace, but at the London Palladium, where they did a dance on stage at the Gala Charity Variety Show. It brought the house down. The team were, however, advised not to give up the day job!

9

Farewell to the Track

When speaking to the National Prayer Breakfast in 1995, Kriss said: 'The Olympics are supposed to be every sportsman's dream but that's only until you become an Olympian. Ambition can be a hard slave master because when you think you get there, someone moves the goal posts. Then you have to make the final, then it's get on the rostrum, and ultimately you have to win the big G.'

That was very much Kriss's mood as he entered 1992. He had become an Olympian – something no one could ever take away from him. He had made it to the final. He had even stepped on the podium. He had an Olympic silver medal – something that the overwhelming majority of Olympians never achieve. It was a lot, but it wasn't enough.

Remember that Kriss's medal collection at this stage included Commonwealth Games gold medals, European Championship gold medals, a World Championship gold medal and an Olympic silver. The Olympic gold was the one that was missing, the one that was needed to complete the set.

The year had begun as usual with a period in California, where Kriss had become accustomed to training in the winter. But what do you do the rest of the day, when training is over? He enrolled at a local university, Azusa Pacific University, which offered him the opportunity of taking a special abridged version of their BA Liberal Arts course.

In 1991 and 1992 he followed courses from January to May, with classes two or three days a week. The course consisted of 60 units and the plan was to take 15 units in 1991, 15 units in 1992 and to return to Azusa after the Olympics to complete the remaining 30 units. (In the end, he didn't complete the course, as business opportunities made it seem unwise to be out of the country for so long.)

The decision to study was more than just something to fill the day. It was a quest for knowledge and a desire to make up for lost time. It also related to the changes in his life resulting from his conversion to Christianity.

> I know I wasted my time as a schoolkid; I never fed my brain. Now I have a thirst for knowledge, for wisdom, to know what life's all about. I've been a Christian for the last four years and it's an integral part of my life. But it throws up a lot of questions and I want to learn so much more. (Mel Watman interview in *Athletics Today*)

The success he had had up to now and the fame and celebrity status was great, but he had to be careful not to let it get in the way of his real purpose. He used this as an illustration in one of his sermons on Mark's Gospel.

> When I was an athlete preparing for the Olympics, I used to get invitations to do all sorts of things – to see the mayor, to come to this dinner, and all of this could have distracted me from my real purpose.
>
> As an athlete, I had to be focused, to be tunnel-visioned. I was focused on the Olympics and on getting to that final in peak condition to do the business. I had to get my priorities right. I had to put in the work, do the training, eat the right things, get enough rest. There was the temptation to let other things deflect me. Many days it would have been easier to go and take tea with the mayor but I had to get down to the track and work. 'Just one more time, Kriss. Let's do that one more time.' Each day I had to reaffirm my commitment to the discipline of my training.

He began the season with four straight wins including the UK Championships, the AAA Championships and a GB v. Kenya match, the fastest of these being 49.16.

Kriss returned from the USA in May while the family stayed in America another four weeks to enable Ashanti and Shakira to complete the school term. Kriss met them at the airport with a BBC driver who was going to take them home as part of the deal for Kriss appearing on a BBC programme. Shakira, who was then four, was surprised that he wasn't coming home with them. 'Where is Papa going?' she asked.

'To the TV studio.'

She was more confused. 'What? We have had to come all the way from America just to see Papa on television?'

While Kriss's focus was firmly on the preparation for the Olympic final, he took a little time out one June Saturday to make a teenage girl's day. Naomi Saunders had attended the Scripture Union One-to-One holiday the previous summer.

As part of the camp, the young people had been invited to express their wildest dream, in 'Jim'll Fix It' style. Naomi wrote, 'I wannabee ... the world's fastest 400 metre runner and win a gold medal at the Olympics.' So it came in June 1992 that Naomi found herself on a track in some remote location near Andover to watch Kriss and Roger Black train. Not content with that, Kriss gave her a quick lesson on hurdling and then she was invited to run a lap or two between Kriss and Roger.

On 6 July, in Lille, exactly one month before the Olympic final, Kriss ran 50.67 for last place. It was a moment of crisis. Was he finally past his best? Would Barcelona prove to be a great embarrassment? Had he gone on a year too long? Did Kriss see it as a moment of crisis?

Not really. To be honest I had a very bad year in 1992. I felt that I wasn't very well and that I did not train very well at all that year. I just stuck to my game plan and hoped I would be in better shape come Barcelona.

He still had a month to be right on the day. A hallmark of a champion is the ability to 'do the business' when it matters, to serve the ace at break-point, to produce the best goods in the final. This is the temperament which enables a performer to peak in the Olympic final, to win a high proportion of the crucial points in a tennis match.

It has to be said that Kriss's track record was in his favour. Up to this point, he had three times broken the UK 400 metres hurdles record – first in the 1990 European Championship final (gold medal), then in the World Championship semi-final and final in 1991 (bronze medal).

He had three more races before the Olympics – he came third in Lausanne in 48.30, second at Crystal Palace in 48.26, and third in Nice in 49.16. At least a platform had been established for the Olympic assault.

Of course, it came good in the end and he picked up an Olympic bronze medal, even if his perhaps unrealistic hopes of gold were dashed. It was, of course, also the fourth time he had broken the UK record.

Shortly before the Olympics, Kriss did a BBC radio programme, *Prayer for the Day*. He chose as his prayer Psalm 8. The interview was recorded at Broadbridge Heath in Horsham, just after he had finished a training session. His comments were another example of the development of his thinking and how he has integrated his Christian faith into all aspects of his life.

Picking up the phrase, 'You made him [Man] a little lower than the heavenly beings and crowned with glory and honour', Kriss commented:

When I see the position that I have, as a person in the human race in the line of God's creation, I feel crowned. Crowned because I have dominion over all the earth and that is such an awesome position to be placed in. Then I realize that God himself came down to earth, that he lowered himself from the high majesty that he had, to be a little lower than the angels, and on the same level as me. When I read that and think of what God has done for me, it is absolutely terrifying... Before I became a Christian, I saw a hierarchy of people and I was at the lower end of the hierarchy or social scale. Now, in becoming a Christian, I realize that God made each and every one of us the work of his hands and we are made equal in the sight of God. That certainly changes the way I interact with people. Regardless of what they are on a social or economic scale, I realize that, if God loves them, how much more should I love them. So in this respect life has changed and given me, I think, a higher opinion of myself. I realize that, regardless of what sort of accent I speak with or what sort of colour I wear, we are all equal in the sight of God.

The bronze medal in the 1992 Olympics did not mark the end of Kriss's Olympic career. There was still one event to come, the 4 × 400 metres relay. As reigning World Champions, much was expected of the UK team, but, as Kriss explains, it was not to be this time.

By the time we came to the relay we had a few tired legs out there and I think, to be honest, we knew that it was not going to be as easy as last time. It was difficult to win in Tokyo but we knew we had the ability to win because the Americans did not have their best team in Tokyo, they were very complacent, they thought they could put any four out to beat us.

This time round the Americans had four guys who could go under 44 seconds and we didn't have one guy who could do that. We'd lost Derek Redmond who was the British record holder, a week earlier. So we knew we were up against it. We were very tired when we got there. I did not think I would be the best man to run this time and tried to get out of it – there were a couple of other young guys who hadn't run during that week. In the end we came third. We felt we should have got silver but that was the measure of how tired we really were.

Athletics Today summed up the race in a headline 'No ifs or butts about US win', a reference to the Britons' claim to have 'kicked the Americans' butts' in the World Championship finals in 1991! This time, Kriss ran the third leg after Roger Black and David Grindley, with John Regis on the anchor leg. The Americans broke the world record with 2:55.74, Cuba were second in 2:59.51 to Britain's 2:59.73.

Kriss finished the season with seven races on the international circuit in Monte Carlo, Sheffield, Cologne, Zurich, Berlin, Copenhagen and Turin. Only once was he under 49 seconds and his results were pretty uninspired – a third, two fourths, three fifths and a sixth.

To be brutally honest, he only ran one outstanding race all season. However, as that race was the Olympic final, it would be hard to criticize his efforts!

The Barcelona Olympics marked a milestone for the Christian presence in the British athletics team. It was at Seoul in 1988 that the Christian group had been launched with just three or four. Since that time, over twenty athletes have attended the gatherings. Most days, a group of about six athletes met together.

As Kriss's Christian faith has grown, he has thought about how it interacts with his sporting talent. Writing in the *Guardian* in the build-up to the 1992 Olympics, he addressed the perceived dichotomy between sport and faith:

> I am that dichotomy. The saying is that Jesus preached a social gospel: love others more than oneself; while sport preaches the selfish: I love me, who do you love?... Sportsmen can easily become disillusioned with what the glamour life has to offer. Vanity, pure vanity, if this is all there is. No, Christians in sport are not two diametri-

cally opposing ideologies but rather the realization that the talent one has is a gift from God for
the benefit of society in the furtherance of the
Gospel, while personally enjoying the spin-offs.

However, there were times when he did not find the
interaction between faith and sport easy to resolve. He
tells this story against himself:

Once my manager came up to me and said,
'Kriss, I've got you two races and there are good
bucks involved.' He gave me the dates, 25 July
and 1 August. The problem was that on 25 July I
had agreed to preach at church and on the second date I had agreed to do something else, for
TV. But when I thought about the races all I
could see was dollar signs.

I spoke to God about it. He said, 'Kriss,
you've an appointment on the 25th.' I said,
'Well, yes, but I could get out of it.' God said:
'Kriss, you've got an appointment on the 25th.' I
heard what God said but I kept thinking about
the dollar signs, about the mortgage I had to pay
off. It was my last year in athletics, one of my last
opportunities to earn that kind of money. So I
rang my minister, Paul Finn, and said, 'Paul, I'm
speaking on 25 July, do you know who is speaking on 18th?' Paul said, 'I am.' I asked if there
was any chance we could do a swap. He said that
would be no problem. So I thought, 'Yes, I can
run the race and get that money and still speak

at church.' God said, 'Kriss, you're out of order. I'll let you speak on the 18th instead of the 25th but you are serving money and not God.'

Guess what happened! The meeting where the lucrative race was got cancelled. That experience showed me that although I read the Bible, pray and witness occasionally, I wasn't all there as a Christian. The Bible says, 'You cannot serve God and money.' I realized that I was putting money before God.

At the end of the 1992 season Kriss made clear that the Barcelona Olympics had been his last major championship. He would run one more season as a farewell. However, his days of serious competition were gone.

A pleasing accolade which came his way in 1992 was the award of an honorary degree by the University of Southampton, in recognition of his achievements and of his connections with the city. Not bad for the boy who had left school without a qualification to his name.

Kriss went off to California as usual just after Christmas for his studies and winter training. In mid-January, reports appeared in the press that he was, in fact, planning a fully competitive 1993 after all.

It all started, as far as one can ascertain, with an article in *Athletics Weekly* by Paul Larkins in January 1993:

Wow, back up a minute! Run that one by me again, Kriss. The first of January is the time to make resolutions and all that, but, if I remember right, and a couple of million BBC Olympic viewers will back me up here, you announced your retirement after the 400 metres hurdles final. And now you're saying you can run a PB [personal best]. What is going on? I think it's time to come clean, Kriss.

But – and it's a big one at that – he might still line up in next summer's World Championships. There are one or two provisos but, given Akabusi's talent, enthusiasm and ability to peak when it matters, they aren't so difficult to envisage.

'There's only one way I'll be going – if I race everybody, beat everybody and run consistently under 47.5,' he says.

So, I think we need a bit of a summary here. Akabusi has retired from major championships unless he goes around Europe beating everybody. To do that, he would probably have to show more speed than ever before. Incidentally he hopes to break new ground by running under 21 seconds for 200 and hopefully follow that up with a PB over the 400 hurdles, possibly a time that would eclipse the European record. A time, by the way, that would win virtually every race out. In the meantime, he has signed to wear Cica shoes, a company that doesn't make spikes. Does that all make sense?

The origins of that article remain a mystery to Kriss. It appears, however, that when the story was put to Mike

Whittingham, he shrugged and said that it wouldn't surprise him if Kriss did change his mind about the 1993 World Championships.

An article in *The Times* was the first I heard of it. At this stage, Kriss did not have his own office as he does now, but used Christians in Sport to deal with fan mail, requests to speak at churches, etc. Occasionally, as Co-Director of Christians in Sport, I would also act as a go-between, setting up press interviews for Kriss. Kriss rang me from the USA to ask me to ring *The Times*, ask where they got the story, and inform them on his behalf that he had not changed his mind and had no intention whatever of seeking selection for the World Championships in Stuttgart. I duly conveyed the message to the Sports Editor of *The Times*.

The same day, David Powell, *The Times*'s Athletics Correspondent, rang me from Rome, having had the message conveyed to him by the Editor. He assured me that he would not have written the story if he had not believed it to be true, and that he certainly had no wish to upset Kriss. Would Kriss like to speak to him to set the record straight? I replied that Kriss regarded it as a 'non-story' and had nothing to say on the matter beyond repeating that it was not true.

Meanwhile, back in sunny California, Kriss was training for what he, at least, knew was going to be a 'lap of honour' type of season. The times of flights to Stuttgart were not on his agenda.

There was one unscheduled race that summer. Kriss had made it clear that he did not want to be considered for any of the major races that season. However, when the selectors decided that Gary Cadogan was not ready for the responsibility of the Europa Cup, Kriss was prevailed upon to come out of retirement.

At first he said, 'No.' Those days were past. Then he was asked again, very much in a spirit of 'Your country needs you.' Reluctantly, he agreed to run. 'Gary rang me up after my selection and told me I was the man for the job. Mind you, I wasn't convinced I was ready, until I had a hectic period learning how to hurdle again' (*Athletics Weekly*).

In the event, he came fourth in 48.73 (his own prediction was that he would run 48.8), in a race won by Stephane Diagana of France in 48.08. Kriss said afterwards, 'I still feel that the decision to pick me has been vindicated. I don't think Gary Cadogan could have done 48.8. At least I've earned six points.'

He also ran in the 4 × 400 metres relay with Duaine Ladejo, John Regis and David Grindley, winning in 3:00.25. Britain finished second overall behind USSR, 128 to 124.

1993 was a year of last races. Kriss's last appearance for Britain in an international was in July in the TSB Challenge, GB v. USA at Meadowbank in Edinburgh. He won his race in 50.45 and received the inevitable standing ovation.

On 8 August 1993, Kriss lined up in the Grand Prix meeting at the Louis II stadium in Monte Carlo. He came sixth in 49.04 behind World Champion Samuel Matete, who won in 47.94, Olympic Champion Kevin Young and the rest. From there they headed for the World Championships in Stuttgart. Kriss went home.

He said of Monte Carlo, 'This is the last time I race these guys. What a great career! I have been privileged to race the best guys in the world for the last four years and I am now looking forward to participating in athletics as a spectator.'

His last race was on 29 August in Sheffield in the McDonald's Games. He came second to Torrance Zellner of the USA, Zellner running 49.2, Kriss running 49.24. *Athletics Weekly* summed up the occasion:

The charismatic hurdler and inspirational 400 metres relay man appeared for his final international-class race wearing dressing-gown and carpet slippers, did half a lap warm-up, finished second in a time faster than his would-be successors have yet achieved, went on a complete lap of honour, then appeared in clown's boots at the meeting's end to wish everyone a fond farewell.

When Kriss was asked to run in the relay in the World Championships, he declined. It was an easy decision as he had made clear all along that Stuttgart did not figure in his plans. He took the opportunity to express disappointment at the British Athletics Federation's lack of co-operation in his final season. 'What bothers me is the idea that my country needs me,' he said.

It's not Britain but the same organization that has told me that it can't help me do a farewell tour of British meetings this summer.

The patriotism is a bit bogus. All I wanted of the British Athletics Federation is to run in front of my home crowd, one last time, against reasonable opposition.

So what happens at Crystal palace on Friday? Andy Norman – the BAF promotions officer – invites the world record holder and the world champion, knowing very well that I wasn't prepared to run at that level.

Not only that but I find out later that without telling me, he put on a B race at the Palace which would have been a perfect way for me to say goodbye. Now Norman's employers want me to help them out.

In September 1993, a dinner was held at the Hilton Hotel to celebrate the career of Kriss Akabusi. It was a fitting tribute to his achievements. Among the guests on the top table with Kriss and Monika were Mr and Mrs David Hemery, whose 22-year British record Kriss had broken.

December 1993 saw another milestone in British athletics: the first UK Christian athletes' conference. When Kriss became a Christian in 1987 he was about the only committed Christian in British athletics. There had been great progress in the intervening years. The presence of Mark McAllister as a travelling pastor, leading Bible studies, became an accepted part of the athletics scene. By 1993, the witness had grown to the point where Richard Nerurkar, Jonathan Edwards and several other athletes could join Kriss for a two-day conference.

At the end of the 1993 season, Kriss hung up his running shoes. He felt the time was right. However, he is convinced that he could have gone on another year or two had he wanted to.

> There is absolutely no doubt in my mind that I could have made the Olympic Games in 1996 had I wanted to. I could still run sub 50 seconds and that would be good enough to get me into the British team, but it would not get me into the final. Perhaps I could even have made the final, but it would have been a far cry from the Akabusi who was on the rostrum in 1992 and I didn't want that.

His fans will be glad he took the decision that he did and did not fall into the trap of keeping going as a shadow of his former self.

10

TV Star

For the majority of sportspeople, the end of the career is a nightmare time to be faced, with an uncertain future. Kriss, however, seemed to step effortlessly from one career to another. TV was part of the secret.

Kriss Akabusi was made for television! His exuberant personality, infectious smile and extraordinary laugh made him a natural. As a successful athlete he was no stranger to media attention, and that gave him a head start in the business. He grasped it with both hands.

Kriss's talent as a performer had emerged while he was still an athlete, manifest in his appearances on *A Question of Sport*, to which he always brought his inimitable sense of fun – such as the time he was to be found half rising from his seat, demanding a point and telling David Coleman not to give him any porkies! Sadly, the scores showed that it was Kriss whose answer was of the porky variety!

Yet when, in 1993, the producer of *The Big Breakfast*, Channel 4's early morning show, invited Kriss to co-present the show with Gaby Roslin, did he realize what he was letting society in for by launching Akabusi the TV star?

Kriss's role was really to be himself, laughing and making exaggerated gestures. Watching videos of the programmes now, Kriss looks a bit wooden and uncertain, compared to the relaxed and easy manner he has since developed. He is very much playing second fiddle to Gaby.

Over the years, his confidence and the range of programmes to which he has contributed has broadened a great deal. Some programmes have been one-offs, some have run and run. The common theme has been Kriss's sense of fun, his great gift of never being embarrassed and being willing to do anything, no matter how silly, if the context is right.

Kriss sees one hazard in this, however:

> The danger is that the media want you always to be the caricature they have created. They see me as this smiling, laughing happy-go-lucky figure, and that is who they want me to be. That is fine; I make a good living out of it. The downside is that it is hard for me to be taken seriously, to move away from this stereotyped role.

Record Breakers

Record Breakers is probably the programme most people now associate Kriss with. His first appearance on Record Breakers was as a member of the 4 × 400 metres relay team in 1991. During the interview, Kriss suddenly started laughing, then the team started laughing, and the interview came to an abrupt end.

When Kriss became a presenter on *Record Breakers*, Cheryl Baker was quick to remind him of that interview and to show it to the viewers. Kriss's first assignment was to report on some water-ski records. His first programme also included interviewing Sally Gunnell and sitting, dinner-jacketed, next to Norris McWhirter of the *Guiness Book of Records*, watching the world's shortest opera, a mere three minutes thirty-four seconds.

Initially, Kriss was a roving reporter, assisting Cheryl and Roy Castle. After Roy's untimely death, Kriss took on a bigger role. Among his assignments for *Record Breakers* have been standing on top of a light aeroplane as it took off and holding hands in mid-air with someone in a similar position on another aeroplane flying above him upside-down. On another occasion, he was snowboarding or, to be more precise, falling off a snowboard. He also took part in an attempt on the world juggling record and a custard-pie throwing contest – he looked a natural!

Fully Booked

One of his greatest successes has been a programme for Children's BBC on Saturday mornings, called *Fully Booked*. In the first series, Kriss's particular assignment was to learn 13 new sports from a celebrity in each sport, with the results presented in a series of short filmed reports.

He tried skating with Torville and Dean, snooker with Stephen Hendry, karting with David Coultard, cycling with Chris Boardman, football with Alan Shearer. He played basketball with the London Towers and American football with the Scottish Claymores. He even finished up at Twickenham to help Kyran Bracken and the England rugby team in their preparation for the World Cup in South Africa.

As a top sportsman in his own right, Kriss enjoyed the exercise and was very respectful of others' talents: 'You get to appreciate the skills that other people have and how hard some other sports are.' His own assessment of the thirteen week series? 'It was good fun. Sometimes I was good at the sport, other times not so good.'

That it was fun could not be denied. After falling in the drink repeatedly while windsurfing (or 'watersurfing' as Kriss more accurately described it) – 'I've spent more time in the water than in the wind.' And after his attempts at canoeing, few could disagree with his conclusion: 'I'm not a water baby!'

Kriss clearly enjoyed skating with Torville and Dean and was excited to see the pair's assessment of his efforts as they held up their cards to register two perfect 6.0s, only to be told, 'Oops, the cards are upside down. We meant 0.9.' His consolation was to take to the ice for a grand finale in the company of Torville and Dean.

The series produced some great one-liners, like David Coultard's 'He may be a famous athlete but he can't drive,' or Torville and Dean's 'Practice makes perfect and you certainly need the practice.' When a simple snooker pot was missed, Stephen Hendry

remarked, 'From that, Kriss, I can see you've learned
...absolutely nothing.' He got in on the act himself,
though. On discovering that Chris Boardman's real
name is 'Miles', Kriss thought that it was appropriate
but wondered if it should not now be changed to
'Kilometre'?

His talents were not always appreciated. After his
day of American football with the Scottish Claymores,
he asked what they felt was his best position in the
game. Without hesitation they brought him the uniform – a cheer-leader's uniform!

Two or three times Kriss co-presented the programme from the studio, getting involved in such zany
stunts as smashing (gramophone) records with a ham-
mer in the company of Morag, the show's resident
highland cow. As Morag put it, 'We're record breakers.' On another occasion he was seen stuffing biscuits
into Dec (of Ant and Dec)'s mouth, in a celebrity eat-
as-many-dry-biscuits-as-you-can competition.

In the last programme of the 1995 series, Morag
the cow presented her highlights of Kriss's sporting
moments, comprising all the bits that went wrong,
showing him falling in the water repeatedly, falling off
a snowboard, falling over on a dry ski slope, coming off
a motocross bike, etc. Rather in the style of a 'goal of
the season', the final programme also included a series
of Kriss' best hee-hawhee-hawhee-haw laughs!

In one of the celebrity phone-ins, Clare Horrill
from Newcastle asked: 'Do you ever stop laughing?'
The answer? 'Ha! ha! ha! Only when I'm eating.
Check her out! Ha! Ha! Ha!'

Generation Game

Kriss has appeared as a celebrity on a range of prime-time TV shows. He appeared in the *Generation Game* as a reluctant hospital patient, who was in a bed which the unfortunate contestants had to make despite his protestations.

At Christmas 1995, accompanied by Monika, Kriss took part in a celebrity episode of Jim Davidson's *Generation Game*. Other contestants were Gloria Hunniford and her son Michael, Eddie Reeves and Vicki Michelle, Jim Bowen and his daughter Sue.

The first game involved dancing with the Ballet Rambert. As Jim Davidson said, some of Kriss's moments seemed more like hurdling than dancing!

Then it was icing a cake, wearing an apron over his dinner jacket. Any good marks were greeted with a chorus of 'All right!' or 'Pump it up!'

The grand finale saw Monika as Little Bo Beep and Kriss as Red Riding Hood in a Panto scene. The scene developed into a panto school lesson and an exchange of corny jokes:

Teacher:	Where was the Magna Carta signed?
Kriss :	At the bottom.
Teacher:	Where is Hadrian's wall?
Monika:	Round Hadrian's house.
Teacher:	Where are the Andies?
Kriss :	At the end of the wristies.

In the end Kriss and Monika were just pipped in the finale by Jim and Sue Bowen, but not before riotous fun had been had by all!

A Question of Sport

When he was competing in track and field, Kriss was a regular panellist in *A Question of Sport*, where his raucous laugh and extrovert personality added greatly to the sense of fun.

In the 1995 Christmas edition, Kriss was the mystery guest, in the guise of Father Christmas. The BBC took him to Lapland to film a sequence, complete with Santa's elves and real reindeer. When Ian Botham guessed correctly the contestants were greeted by the famous laugh and a 'Well, did you get it, guys?'

Other Programmes

Kriss's ability to take over in a situation when he was really supposed to be a guest was well illustrated on *Alive and Kicking*. Andy Peters sneezed on camera during his conversation with Kriss. Kriss jumped in, 'Alright. Next time I am on camera I am going to sneeze. You are my role model, Andy. Hello, Kriss Aaashoo! That has got to be on *Auntie's Bloomers*.' Andy Peters gave up his attempt to conduct a serious interview at this point, with Kriss continuing to imitate poor Andy's sneeze.

Kriss did a series for TyneTees called *Big Burst*, a programme to encourage young people to do sport and see that it could be fun. He even got to meet Gladiator Falcon!

Eamonn Holmes, interviewing Kriss on *Oddballs* in 1995, introduced Kriss in an interesting way: 'He has Olympic, Commonwealth Games and European Championship medals in his drawer, certainly nothing to laugh about but I'm sure he will. Ladies and gentlemen, Kriss Akabusi.'

As Kriss took his seat and the applause died down, Holmes continued, 'You really are a miserable git, aren't you!' To prove the point Kriss fell about laughing.

The 'God-Slot'

With his high-profile Christian faith, Kriss is a natural to present and take part in religious programmes. He brings a sense of fun and the potential for wider audiences to the 'God-slot'. He feels that such programmes are part of his Christian life and he is happy to contribute to them when it seems appropriate.

One programme that Kriss was delighted to be involved in was *Summer Sunday*, a series of four Sunday morning programmes in 1995. The programmes aimed to unpack what Christianity is all about. It was described by the *Observer* as 'an attempt at hip God-slot programming'.

The programmes were full of fun, lively music and interviews. They were presented on location in Portsmouth, Scarborough, Covent Garden and Cyprus. Kriss worked with Steve Chalke of the Oasis Trust as co-presenter. The programme was a good opportunity to share his faith in a relevant, upbeat way.

In early 1996, he took part in a special *Songs of Praise* programme in which Sally Magnusson interviewed Kriss and Jonathan Edwards about their sporting achievements and their journey to faith. It was hardly what you would call a dull programme. When Sally asked the first question, Jonathan and Kriss collapsed laughing. The tone for the programme was set!

He was invited by London Weekend Television to co-host, with Gloria Hunniford, a Sunday Morning programme called *Sunday People*. The approach of the programme was multi-faith and included a wide range of religious experiences. Kriss told the producers that, as a committed Christian, he could not endorse such an approach:

As a Christian I believe that God has shown us absolute truth in the person of Jesus Christ. I cannot accept that all religions are equally valid in this respect. Therefore I could not be an uncritical observer to a show where there are moral conflicts with the basic tenets of Christianity. That is to say, I would be unwilling to be seen endorsing or giving credence to a pantheistic view of faith and religion. I am all for Christians having a look at other faiths and the mechanics thereof but I do feel their presuppositions need to be examined from a biblical perspective. In short if we were saying all paths lead

117

to God and all faiths have equal validity I, as a Christian, would feel my faith compromised.

If he took part in the programme it would be as a Christian, representing the Christian viewpoint. In the end, someone else presented the programme.

Gotcha

As an established TV presenter, Kriss from time to time gets invitations to be a guest presenter on a range of programmes. One such invitation came out of the blue in 1993, for a programme called *Off the Beaten Track*, which purported to be an alternative holiday programme for BBC2.

Kriss was told that his role was not just to present the programme but also to be something of an investigative journalist. He was to put together a report about a 'personal development centre' run by a man called Roger. People went there for a weekend to renew themselves, to cut themselves off from the real world.

On arrival, Kriss and the team were a little surprised to see a Cadillac parked round the back of the house and to notice that Roger seemed to spend most of his time on a mobile phone. So much for being cut off from the world! In view of this, the producer encouraged Kriss to push Roger hard on some of these issues.

Kriss was invited to join in with some of those who were spending a period at the centre. First he joined a group who were 'vacuuming their minds'. He was asked by Malachi, who was leading the session, to take a moment to release the tension and to cleanse the body by caressing his leg gently like a vacuum cleaner. He would feel the tension leave him.

Asked by the producer to speak to camera, Kriss was for once almost lost for words. He stuttered and then said: 'Well, Malachi is very sincere and has really got into this...Well, it's very different. I don't feel any better for it but perhaps I haven't entered into it 100 per cent.'

The second experience saw him lying on a bed having a crystal held in front of him. Again, while Moonstone (the girl who was holding the crystal) said that she could feel a lot of energy, Kriss was unconvinced.'I have to be honest, I didn't feel anything but perhaps I'm not tuned in. It didn't move for me.' Kriss then did a very serious piece to camera: 'I confess to being a sceptic at this moment. I don't really understand what is going on here but we are going to find out.'

Kriss then got into a heated debate after being told to close his eyes and touch a sensitive part of his body, to love himself and to marry himself. He was told to go deeper. Kriss snapped back, 'I don't want to go deeper. I don't have the mindset that allows me to believe you can marry yourself. I cannot. I am married to my wife.'

As the filming continued, Kriss was becoming distinctly uneasy. As a Christian, he was not happy with what was going on. It all seemed a bit New-Age to him. He wondered whether or not he should be there. Was he compromising his faith?

The producer then told Kriss to ask about charges. Roger was reluctant to answer, but as Kriss pressed him he gave a figure of £450, the cheque to be payable to Roger himself. Kriss and the producer were delighted, feeling that they had caught Roger out. 'We have got a bit of an exclusive,' they told each other.

Then Kriss was taken to watch the 'regeneration' of a guest. A group of people were chanting; gradually the chanting became more audible: 'Got, G-o-t, G-o-ot.' Then the guest who was being regenerated stuck out a hand with the Gotcha Oscar and said, 'Gotcha!' Kriss stared, dazed for a moment, then laughed and screamed, 'I don't believe it!' and 'What a stitch-up!'

Back in the studio he was still laughing, but also shouting to Noel Edmonds, 'I'll get you back!'

This is Your Life

No amount of TV appearances prepared Kriss for the events of Thursday 27 April 1995. Kriss was returning from Australia, where he had been combining a family holiday with some work for Record Breakers.

On arrival at Heathrow, he was surprised to be greeted by his fellow Record Breakers presenter, Cheryl Baker. He said, 'Hi!' and then noticed that Cheryl was holding up a card with his name on it. Suddenly, four others appeared holding cards with words on them. Slowly, he read, 'KRISS AKABUSI, THIS IS YOUR LIFE.' He was gobsmacked!

'I can't believe it!' he said. 'I'm lost for words. I'm not normally lost for words but I am this time!'

After a day 'imprisoned' in a hotel – lest he should meet any of the others who were taking part in the programme – Kriss was taken to the BBC TV Centre for the programme recording. On the stage he was delighted to see not only Monika and the children but also Monika's family who had travelled over from Germany for the programme and a number of friends and associates.

Seated just behind Kriss was his super-efficient PA, Liz Bednall, who had masterminded much of the event, liaising with Thames TV (who made the programme for the BBC), making sure Kriss would be where he was supposed to be and helping draw up the list of guests – all this without Kriss suspecting a thing.

The programme was a fitting tribute to Kriss's achievements and helped him relive many memories. The one aspect of Kriss's life which was conspicuous by its absence was his Christian faith, the only reference being Daley Thompson's comment on his enthusiasm for the church. Thompson also shared a story, backed by photographic evidence, about how Kriss, having lost a game of cards with fellow athletes, had to go for a late-night swim. Kriss reacted to this by jumping up on the chair to do an impersonation of Daley. On a more serious note, Daley paid tribute to Kriss's achievement of reaching the top in two events – 400 metres flat and 400 metres hurdles. He added, 'I'm only glad he didn't have time to do the decathlon [Daley's own event] as well!'

Several significant people from Kriss's early life took part in the programme, including his former social workers Jocelyn and Steve Longworth. Jocelyn embarrassed Kriss by reminding him that he had introduced her to Monika as his sister, in case Monika thought she was a girlfriend!

Shirley and Brian Martin, who ran the children's home in Enfield, recalled how they were trying to adopt a child and getting nowhere. Kriss decided to take action and organized all sixteen children to march off to the offices of Islington Social Services as a protest. The Martins were eventually able to adopt a baby girl.

An interesting aspect of the show was how people addressed Kriss, reflecting the period of his life when they met him. Those who went right back to his childhood still called him 'Kezie', his army mates called him 'Aki' or 'Akismith', his army nickname, and only people who had met him in adult civilian life called him 'Kriss'.

One thing that Kriss really appreciated was the tribute from the world's greatest ever hurdler, Ed Moses, who said: 'I would like to say congratulations to you, Kriss Akabusi, on your accomplishments in your career. I remember in 1985 or 1986 when you first came to train at the University of California in Irvine and we became friends. Congratulations from one champion to another on your victory, winning a medal in Barcelona. I wish you all the best in your career and the best in life, to you and your family.'

The programme would have been incomplete without a reference to the 1991 relay victory. Of the team, Derek Redmond was in the studio and John Regis and

Roger Black contributed a filmed interview from America. Their contribution recalling the 1991 World Championship relay gold medal took the form of a dialogue and went something like this:

Black: I remember that day, John. I ran a magnificent first leg. I passed that baton on to Derek Redmond and he was just majestic as he gave that baton on to you.

Regis: He certainly was and I ran the leg of history, I was so quick. But when I passed the baton on to you, Kriss, you seemed to trip, stumble and fall across the line and still receive the acclaim of the crowd!

Both: And you've never let us forget it!

The biggest surprise of the night for Kriss came when Michael Aspel told him that his father had made the journey to London for the programme. 'No way!' exclaimed Kriss, then hugged his father, who was seeing his grandchildren for the first time.

Afterwards the BBC laid on a party for all those who participated in the programme. For Kriss, it was a wonderful reunion with people who, in some cases, he had not seen for many years. At times he was – uncharacteristically – lost for words. While he was the centre of attention, he was not in control and was often taken by surprise when new guests were announced. The unexpected appearance of his father was the icing on the cake.

11

Would the Real Kriss Akabusi Please Stand Up?

Kriss has made the transition to life after athletics with remarkably few problems. Kriss describes himself these days as a 'Media and PR Consultant'. TV, media, public speaking engagements, Superschools, Duke of Edinburgh's Award Scheme, panto, and so on now fill his days. Just as he felt that the crucial switch from the 400 flat to the 400 metres hurdles in 1986 – which changed him from an average international athlete to one of real world class – was of God, so he sees God's hand in the development of his life off the track.

> The times when I have really grown in my own life have been moments of abrupt change. For example, I was in the children's home and then I joined the Army, an abrupt change but I flourished. In athletics, I changed from 400 flat to 400 hurdles, an abrupt change but it transformed my career. Christianity hit into my life. Boom! An abrupt change but I turned round and became a changed person in an instant.

There are several aspects to his new life, the sum of which might reveal the real Kriss Akabusi.

Kriss Akabusi the Sportsman

Kriss is first and foremost a sportsman. Even though his career is over he believes that his roots are in sport. It is as a sportsman that people still think of him. His fame, his wealth, his opportunities, all are built on the platform of his sporting achievements.

Does he miss track and field?

> Nothing will ever take the place of being a competitive athlete and going to the Olympic Games and knowing this is the day to perform. I've done that. It was a really great part of my life, but there is more to life than running round the track. I don't miss the competitive side of athletics but I miss the camaraderie.

When Kriss began to take his athletics seriously, he was told by his German coach that he needed to give it priority and stop turning up unfit to train because of injuries picked up in other sports. Since retiring from athletics he has taken up other sports with great enthusiasm. He plays football regularly for the church team. He had a go at basketball with the Worthing Bears. He is becoming a fanatical tennis player. When he spoke at the National Prayer Breakfast in 1995, he was introduced as 'a man who has enjoyed great sporting success but who has never beaten Roger Black at tennis!' He is pretty competitive on the tennis court. 'Just for fun' is not in the Akabusi sporting vocabulary.

Not a lot of people know this, but Kriss once had a trial for Leyton Orient football club. It didn't work out but he is a regular member of the Southampton Christian Fellowship team on Saturday mornings. His own assessment is, 'Although I play several sports I am so unfit compared to what I used to be.'

Kriss Akabusi the Celebrity

Chambers Dictionary defines celebrity as 'the condition of being celebrated; fame, notoriety; a person of distinction or fame'. A celebrity is someone who has been put in the public eye either by virtue of their performance or their business. There are different levels of celebrity, but perhaps a good yardstick is to be a household name, with half the people in any group knowing who you are.

It is virtually impossible in today's society to be a celebrity without being on TV regularly. The famous stage actor becomes a celebrity when he appears on a TV soap. Take Judy Simpson, for example. As an athlete she won a Commonwealth gold medal, a European bronze medal and came fifth in the Olympics, but it took Gladiators to make her a celebrity!

What are the pluses and minuses of being a celebrity? How does Kriss see it?

The essence of being a celebrity is that you can earn a living by being who you are and just doing what you do and by being yourself. A nice aspect of it is that you can bring pleasure to someone just by saying hello, taking a moment to speak to someone, signing an autograph, having a photo taken with someone.

On the other hand, many people can remember the day they met so-and-so and he was arrogant or rude.

With the privilege comes the responsibility. Like it or not, if you are a celebrity you are a role model, whether for good or bad. Like it or not, people look at the celebrity and pick the good or the bad points. That is certainly a lesson that the advertising people have learnt. If Gary Lineker eats Jones's crisps, so should you. If Brand X is Jack Charlton's favourite breakfast cereal, then it is the one for you too. If Eric Cantona wears that brand of trainers, shouldn't you too?

The negative side of being a celebrity is the lack of privacy. The moment you step out of your front gate, you are public property. Everyone thinks they own you, that they are entitled to some of your time.

I am aware of where I come from. I think there is a danger that you start to believe your own PR, to think you are something special. There is no doubt that my popularity has exceeded my achievements. In pure hardware and medals there are athletes who have achieved far more than I have but have not had the recognition. You become a creation of the media. It becomes circular. The more they write about you, the more famous you become. The more famous you become, the more they write about you.

Kriss Akabusi the Businessman

Kriss earns his living by being Kriss Akabusi. People like to meet him. People like to hear him speak. People pay him to promote their cause.

For three years, Kriss worked as part-time promotions officer for the Duke of Edinburgh's Award Scheme. The scheme has been in existence for 37 years in 52 countries and has helped some two million people in the 14–25 age group to learn skills of self-discipline and leadership through community service, physical education and expeditions. The scheme enables young people to gain self-confidence and develop a sense of responsibility for others, attributes of which Kriss – especially bearing in mind his own teenage years – thoroughly approves.

At first I thought it was only for young, white, middle-class people and I am none of these. But when I saw the range of things they were doing I jumped at the chance to help.

It was a partnership of mutual respect. Michael Hobbs, director of the scheme said, 'Kriss was the perfect choice. As well as his blazing integrity and his ideals, he has an ability to enthuse young people and talk to them in a language they understand.'

At the moment, Kriss works with Pritt Super-schools, an organization that promotes health and well-being for young people in schools. The emphasis is on participation in sport for all, but they also give grants to talented young people to help them develop their talents.

Alan Hubbard of the *Observer* once wrote of Kriss: 'Nobody has a bad word to say about Akabusi except, perhaps, one or two athletics promoters who have found to their cost that in negotiating appearance money his Christian beliefs do not always find him charitable.'

Kriss's reaction?

Fair comment! But don't forget that the Bible tells us to be as wise as serpents but as harmless as doves. People expect me to be gentle in nego-tiations but in fact I am very hard and people are surprised by that.

Kriss has never had any problems with tough negotiat-ing. Perhaps it is a legacy of his childhood but he does not easily trust people. He is always wary of being tak-en for a ride or of selling himself short.

Kriss Akabusi the Thespian

A thespian is a tragic actor. On reflection, that may be quite a good way to describe Kriss!

129

At Christmas 1994, he was invited to be part of a pantomime, *Dick Whittington* in Southampton. He had the opportunity of playing in a very strong cast which included Rosemarie Ford (*Generation Game*), Lesley Joseph (*Birds of a Feather*), John Nettles (*Bergerac*) and Windsor Davies.

The part was a character called Ak-a-a-b-u-u-s-s-s-i who appeared when King Rat conjured up an Olympic athlete. Kriss ran around the stage like a demented hare and was constantly told to 'keep still' by other characters in the show. It was quite a small part in which his role involved looking up a lady's skirt, kidnapping two ladies and some general clowning around. As another character said, 'We brought Akabusi along to help us get over any hurdles that get in our way.' Groan, groan!

Always keen to diversify his career, Kriss was enthusiastic about giving it a try. His initial reaction was favourable: 'I thoroughly enjoyed it. I don't like playing a baddy though. Being used to being "Mr Nice-Guy", it takes a bit of getting used to, being booed and hissed!'

He was delighted on being told by the manager that the theatre's market research indicated that his presence was the major attraction to the paying public. He was, however, less than chuffed to discover that he was one of the poorest paid members of the cast.

In December 1995 and January 1996, he was again in *Dick Whittington*, this time in Woking. He found six weeks a long run, particularly as his part had not developed at all. While the money was better than the previous year, being unavailable for other work for the whole of January involved turning down some more lucrative opportunities.

A certain tension also arose between the cast and the management over the question of tickets for the show. Management declined to make any complimentary tickets available for friends of the cast. Thus, when Kriss brought his family to see the show, he had to purchase tickets for them. However, on other occasions he was expected to put himself out promoting the show – including a 300-mile round trip to Birmingham for a TV show – with no extra payment.

Kriss Akabusi the Nigerian Chief

It is easy to forget that Kriss Akabusi is Nigerian. He was born in Paddington of Nigerian parents. As already described, Kriss was initially horrified at the prospect of returning to Nigeria with his mother. Moreover, his change of name from the Nigerian 'Kezie' to the Anglicized 'Kriss' was in effect a rejection of his heritage.

Nonetheless, his father is a chief of several villages and as his father's first born, one day Kriss will inherit his father's title as Duru Ojiaku III. How does he view that?

The older I get, the more important my Nigerian heritage has become. When I was a kid it was totally irrelevant. Now I see it as my culture, my background, my heritage. It is also important for

me that my children understand and talk about
their Nigerian heritage. I want to be buried in
Nigeria.

There is a dichotomy. I am British. I have a
British attitude to life and point of view. I have
lived virtually all my life in Britain. The Nigerian
culture is quite different. Yet when I go to Nigeria, I instantly feel at home. My father's village in
Nigeria is a million miles from the life I am used
to in the UK, yet when I go there I feel that this
is where I belong, I feel empathy with the place.

It is hard to explain but I am British but not
English. I am also Nigerian. I am proud to be
Nigerian. I don't think I could have said that 25
years ago.

As my father's first born, one day I will inherit
my father's title. If I do not accept it, it would
pass out of our family which I would not want. I
look at the line and how the title has come into
the family and realize that it is an important part
of my heritage. So it is a duty and a responsibility
as much as anything else.

If I appointed one of my uncles as regent to
rule by proxy then I could continue to live in
England and just go back to Nigeria on regular
visits. In Nigeria I am like part of the landed
gentry.

When Kriss's father Daniel came to England in 1995
for the *This is Your Life* programme, an incident
occurred that illustrated some of the cultural gaps.

Daniel came to stay a few days with Kriss and his family. One evening they had a barbecue and in a fashion that is very common in the UK in the 1990s, Kriss cooked on the barbecue while Monika organized salads, etc. Astounded, Daniel asked Kriss, 'Doesn't your wife do anything? You go out and earn the money and still you have to cook your own food!'

Kriss Akabusi the Speaker

Speaking is something that has always come naturally to Kriss, and, at the moment, speaking at corporate sales conferences represents a significant amount of his income.

Whether speaking in school assemblies, giving motivational talks to business conferences, representing the Duke of Edinburgh's Award Scheme or Superschools, Kriss's message is the same: 'Work hard to achieve all you can, but ultimately without God you won't find meaning and satisfaction to life.'

Invitations to speak in interesting places come his way. A few years ago, he was invited to address the Oxford Union. He gave an account of his life and experience and then answered questions. At one stage, he got quite excited and jumped up on a chair to make his point better. To the general amusement of the audience, the President of the Union told him that under an ancient rule of the Union he was liable for a ten-shilling fine for standing on the chair!

He also took part in a debate at Cambridge University about the existence of God. Opposing him was

Nicholas Walter, a leading rationalist. The debate revolved around the motion, 'This house believes that without God life is meaningless'. Kriss argued his case cogently and enjoyed the lively debate with people who disagreed with him, both in the formal debate and individually over a glass of wine afterwards.

In November 1995, Kriss found himself addressing the National Prayer Breakfast at the Queen Elizabeth II Conference Centre, situated across the road from the Houses of Parliament. Among those taking part were The Lord Chancellor, Lord Mackay of Clashfern, Betty Boothroyd, Speaker of the House of Commons and Kate Hoey, MP and former international athlete. Kriss was the main speaker.

He took as his theme 'Many parts, one body'. He began:

> Some people are born into positions of authority while others into mediocrity, some into power and wealth, others into subservience and poverty, but the Bible says, 'God created us equal, male and female he created us. In his own image, he made us' (Genesis 1:27). There appears here a contradiction either in the biblical precept or my existential concept. However the Good Book goes on to give an explanation for the inequality we see around us. And I quote Paul the apostle:
>
> "From one man he made every nation of men, that they should inhabit the whole earth; and he determined the times set for them and the exact places where they should live. God did

this so that men would seek him and perhaps reach out for him and find him, though he is not far from each one of us. 'For in him we live and move and have our being." (Acts 17:22–28)

He continued to talk about his life, contrasting being born into a position of authority, as the first-born son and hereditary heir to an Ibo Chief, with a childhood filled with anything but pomp and ceremony. He described his army days, his discovery of athletics and his progress from army recreational runner to Olympian. He talked about his year of change in 1986. He drew on the experience of the 1991 relay victory as a supreme example of teamwork.

He finished:

God has made us equal but he has also made us different. Those differences are not meant to glorify us as individuals but to magnify the group as a whole. By committing our different skills to the advancement of the common good, we fulfil the second commandment, Love your neighbour as yourself. To be the greatest we have to serve all. And through this we find that although we are different, we are all equal, many parts but one body.

(I would to place on record that I won a bet with Kriss at the Prayer Breakfast that he would be approached by at least five people who would ask him to come and speak at their school, church, meeting or whatever. This is a feature of every occasion where Kriss speaks.)

Kriss Akabusi the Preacher

In the early years of his Christian life, Kriss used to go out speaking in churches a great deal. He wanted to share his faith and this seemed a good way of doing it. After a while, he came to the conclusion that this was not the best use of his time.

> When I first became a Christian I did a great deal of speaking at churches up and down the country. I was so keen to tell people about Jesus that I didn't want to turn anything down.
>
> Looking back, however, I feel that many of these opportunities could have been better utilized as many of those attending were already Christians. After the service, rather than telling people about Jesus, I found myself talking athletics and signing autographs. I also realized that these people didn't know the real me. I now feel more comfortable speaking in my own church where people know me and can judge if my walk matches my words.
>
> I believe God is primarily calling me to be a witness where I am – to the people I meet in my line of business and through the media, rather than to be a celebrity Christian speaking at a different church each Sunday.

In September 1993, Kriss preached at the Waterfront Church in Southampton at the Novotel. The church met in a hotel to be more accessible to people who were not regular churchgoers.

Ruth Gledhill, Religion Correspondent of *The Times*, featured the occasion in her 'At Your Service' review in the newspaper. The column is written in the style of a restaurant review, with stars up to a maximum of five being awarded for the sermon, the liturgy, the architecture, the music, etc. The sermon got four stars, with the following comment:

> The congregation was transfixed by an eloquent talk from the athlete Kriss Akabusi, whose winning ingredients were the willingness to laugh at himself and an astonishing turn of speed as he raced through his complex and gripping life story.

The story was accompanied by two pictures, one of which showed Kriss standing with one leg high in the air, acting out the Olympic hurdles race!

I had accompanied Kriss to the service that evening, only to find myself the butt of one of Kriss's stories during the sermon. The story went something like this:

> I was once preaching with Stuart sitting behind me. I preached too long. In exasperation someone in the congregation threw a large hard object at me. I ducked but it hit Stuart and knocked him down. People rushed to help him and as he was in good hands I carried on preaching. Stuart was groaning on the floor and someone asked him if

he was all right. 'No,' he replied, 'I can still hear him!'

The service made an impact on Ruth Gledhill, as the conclusion to her article shows:

> At the end of his sermon, he asked those of us who considered ourselves Christians to stand up – the kind of request that normally inspires me to run for the nearest door. About a dozen remained seated but I for once was unable to withstand the challenge when confronted with such a muscular Christianity.

Afterwards, Kriss stayed around, signed autographs and chatted to people. Even after he had finally said his good-byes, he was button-holed in the car park by a student who came up to him and said, 'Well, Kriss, I've listened to what you had to say. Tell me, how can you reconcile your faith with having such a big car? If I was a Christian I would give half my money to the poor and do all the good things I could think of.'

Kriss takes up the story:

> At first, I wanted to be like Jesus and not answer him. Then I said to him: 'How much do you earn?' He told me. So I said, 'I presume that you give half of that to the poor.' Of course he didn't. That guy had completely missed the point of the message that evening. He hadn't come to hear about Christ. He had come to pick up some

apologetic argument to strengthen his own position. He didn't have the integrity to understand his own position.

Kriss's preaching is now more or less confined to his own church. He is sure that this is right and about his reasons:

> I have taken as my role model, Jesus. Jesus taught at synagogues where the common man was permitted to discuss the meaning of Scripture. There Christ's lifestyle, as well as his message, was under scrutiny. He took his ministry to the city streets and roads of Palestine, to homes and fields and to anywhere else the common people might be found.
>
> To fulfil the first criteria, I teach at my home church on a regular basis where my walk as well as my talk can be evaluated. In attempting to accommodate the second, I use the opportunity my secular platform gives me to weave into my messages of motivation, pearls of wisdom gleaned from the Bible.
>
> No evangelistic crusades, just apply your faith to your daily work, rest or play.

Recently, at the Southampton Christian Fellowship, he preached his way through Mark's gospel. The series was based on 'my experience of reading Mark's gospel and trying to live out the message of the book in my own life'. These sermons were published earlier this year by the Bible Reading Fellowship under the title *On your Mark*.

In 1995, Kriss was invited to be on the panel which judged *The Times* Preacher of the Year panel. He declined, but the fact that he was asked is at least evidence of his progress as a preacher.

Kriss Akabusi the Family Man

When Ashanti was born, Kriss admits that he struggled to be a father. Having no real experience of his parents during his childhood he struggled to let Ashanti be emotionally as well as physically close.

Years later, he is comfortable in the role of father. His work takes him away a lot, but nothing is more important than spending time with the family, taking the children to school, collecting them from school, attending their sports days, and so on. In all these ways he is a normal father and family man. In some respects, because of the chaotic pattern of work, it is easier for him to schedule attendance at the sports day than it is for the 9 to 5 office worker.

Kriss Akabusi the Dog Owner

There is a sign on the wall in the Akabusi household: 'HE'S BIG, HE'S BAD, HE'S MAD. HE'S DILLINGER.' Dillinger is Kriss's Doberman. He spends much of his day lying in the back of Kriss's Range Rover, a pretty expensive kennel, really! Kriss contributed the following to a book on celebrity pets:

Dillinger is my second Doberman and I have had him for almost two years. He was born on my birthday, November 28 1993, and was a birthday present.

His pedigree name is Blitzgeist, which means lightning spirit, and boy, believe me, he is true to his name! Everything he does is fast. He runs fast, he eats fast and he barks fast. You may say, 'How does a dog bark fast?' Well, he doesn't go 'Woof! Woof! Woof!' He goes 'WooooOOOf!!!'

On a more serious note, my dog is very big and powerful. He would not do anybody any harm but he is obviously capable of it as he weighs more than seven stone and could be quite aggressive. That is why I think it is important to have dogs well trained and it is imperative that you have control over a dog this size. Dillinger is in the top class at Locksheath and District training club.

He is a great friend and is always really happy to see me. He is great fun and life wouldn't be the same without him.

Kriss Akabusi the Public Christian

Being a Christian is a vital part of Kriss's life. Because he is in the public eye, he inevitably ranks with Cliff Richard as one of the most high-profile Christians in the UK.

It is a privilege and a responsibility. On the one hand, there are great opportunities in the media to speak clearly about his faith. On the other hand, he worries at times about something happening which would damage not only his personal reputation but that of the gospel and the Christian faith.

He sees himself as a Christian role model. As he puts it, 'Part of the fruit of the spirit is joy, and God wants me to express my joy in the best way so people can see you can be a Christian and still have fun.'

An example of this came in early 1996. The Church of England Doctrine Commission had produced a report which had affirmed the traditional view of Hell. The report stated: 'Hell is a reality and everyone faces a day of judgement'. The Press Association contacted Kriss: 'Did he believe in Hell? What were his views?' He was in no doubt about what he believed on the issue, but should he comment? He was not a member of the Church of England, and was concerned not to say something which could be misused. A tabloid headline, 'Akabusi Slams Church of England' would have been helpful to no one.

In the end, he decided that he was happy to be quoted as saying that he too believed in the reality of hell and in judgement for everyone.

When the National Lottery was launched, Kriss was invited to present a winning cheque to some lucky winners. The fee on offer was good and he did it without much thought. However, when he discussed it with his advisory panel – a group of five Christian friends who meet him every month to pray for him and to give him advice as Christian brothers – he reconsidered it. He decided that he did not want to be publicly associated with the Lottery and that he would not present cheques to winners in future. As he was asked to promote scratch cards as well, this was an occasion when following his conscience was costly to his pocket.

Some people are not happy with Kriss in this role. When he produced a book, *Kriss Akabusi on Track with the Bible*, with chapters on Jesus, sin, forgiveness, prayer, death, etc., it was generally well received. One reviewer, however, wondered 'Why we ask people to write a Christian book just because they are famous in other areas of life?'

Kriss answered that question in the foreword of the book containing his sermons on Mark:

> My answer is simple. I am a Christian with firmly held views and beliefs. I am often called to give an account of those views by the public, be it from business, universities, schools or the sports field for the faith that I have within me. It is my belief that God calls different people at different times to prominence, to shine the spotlight on them for just that reason. It is my ministry.

There are many different Kriss Akabusis or more correctly many facets or manifestations of his personality. Peter Nichols once said of him that he was 'in great demand but with no trace of self-importance'. A fitting tribute.

12

A Day in the Life of Kriss Akabusi

As an international athlete, Kriss's days were mapped out before him. The Olympic final was on 6 August 1992. Everything for months before was geared to being in peak form at just the right time. As a soldier, he followed the timetable imposed on him by his superiors.

When the athletics career ended, he was free for the first time to organize his life as he wished. He would determine his schedule the way he wanted it. Kriss admits to feeling the pressure in the early days:

> After I retired from athletics I was very, very busy. I had to try to get my physical life in order, to establish a new career. I needed to make some dosh. I wanted to make my family happy, make things happen. The rat race is a hard taskmaster.

There was the understandable temptation to do too much. He was saying 'yes' to everything – in case, if he said 'no', he wasn't asked again. Gradually, it settled down and he worked out how much he needed to do to keep the wolf from the door and began to recognize the type of thing to which he should say, 'no, thank you'.

There are no *typical* weeks in his life, but the following is a *real* week – from November 1995 – which shows how his time is taken up.

Monday	10.00	Business meeting at home.
	2.00	Tennis
Tuesday	8.30	RE lesson in local school, speak and answer questions
	12.30	Health Education Council meeting in London Travel to Manchester
Wednesday	9.30	Superschools in Manchester
	1.00	Superschools in Manchester
Thursday	11.30	Youth Charter reception, Manchester
Friday	10.30	Piano lesson
	5.00	Fly to Belfast for BBC Children in Need
Saturday	8.15	Fly home, hoping to arrive in time to play football for church team
Sunday		Day with family

After he stopped competing as an athlete, Kriss set up his own office where he employs a secretary/administrator, Liz Bednall, to look after his affairs. He also has a business manager to look after some aspects of his commercial activities and a floor manager to co-ordinate events on the day.

Between his engagements, he will pop into the office to read the post and check with Liz what needs his attention. For every event that makes it into his schedule there are ten which do not. If he said 'yes' to even half the invitations he receives, he would never see his family at all.

He receives invitations to speak at a public school chapel, a Pentecostal church in Scotland, a Methodist church 150th anniversary, a Salvation Army weekend in Norwich, a big youth event in Northern Ireland, a church in Jersey.

Would he like to be part of charity 'It's a Knock-out' in Inverness, or a charity fun day somewhere else, a local charity road race? Has he time to attend the celebrity fashion show for the Rwanda famine appeal, a teddy bears' picnic for needy children, to open a charity shop in Yorkshire, to support Blandford No Smoking Day, to help raise funds for various building projects, to be at McDonald's McHappy Day, to contribute a grace to a cathedral organ appeal book of graces?

Could an international advertising campaign use his photo? Has he time for the London Taxi Drivers Fund for underprivileged children? Could he launch the South-West Hampshire Materials Recovery Facility or attend the a youth crime seminar? What about opening a new sports hall at a school in High Wycombe or presenting prizes in Ipswich, Colchester or Bristol? How about a fun run around Norwich? Could he attend a pre-race pasta party for runners for charity in the London Marathon?

What, Kriss asks, have the above all got in common? Answer: They all feel that the presence of Kriss Akabusi is essential to the success of their cause.

Since becoming a Christian, Kriss has always read the Bible with great enthusiasm. He usually rises early to ensure that it is not crowded out of his schedule.

Kriss receives many questionnaires as a result of young people's school projects. They ask questions such as – What do you eat before races? How often do you train? Which opponent do you fear? One food science project wanted him to make a note of everything that he ate and drank for a week! Most of these seem to come in the build-up to the World Championships or the Olympic Games.

The following is a real letter that Kriss received in March 1995:

Dear Kriss

My name is Alexander I am 8 years old and I go to Holy Trinity School in Surrey. I am a year 3 and this term we have to do a biography and I chose to do it on you.

I have put down a list of questions to ask and would be very happy if you could answer them. If you have anything else you could add to help me write a biography, please do so.

Thank you for your help

Alexander

Within the limited time available, Kriss tries to help and to answer as many questionnaires of this type as he can.

The schedule is often punishing. Does he ever wake up and think, I can't face driving to Manchester today?

Not really. I am a bit of a loner. I enjoy driving and travelling. I enjoy driving, thinking things through, listening to the radio, etc. I would hate to have to do a long journey with someone else in the car but basically I enjoy my work and what I do.

Another activity to be fitted into his schedule is interviews. If it is a major feature, it will be arranged in advance and time allocated. Equally, there are many occasions when Kriss turns up for an appointment and the local radio station or the local paper want to 'have a quick word with him'.

Doesn't it drive him mad being asked the same questions every time?

You do get asked the same questions but not necessarily in the same order and you don't get asked all the same questions every time. The audience is different and you have to remind yourself that it is fresh for the person who is hearing it.

What I find difficult is when I go back somewhere – for example to a school where half the people have heard me you before and know what you are going to say. That can be difficult and a struggle to be really fresh.

Mostly, Kriss has enjoyed good relations with the press and had good publicity. Of course there have been some exceptions. In October 1991, the *Today* newspaper claimed an exclusive, under the title, 'My family shame by sprinter Kriss'. The article began: 'Star hurdler Kriss Akabusi has revealed that his royal Nigerian family accused him of shaming them by marrying a white girl.' The article was meant to look like an exclusive, new revelation, but in reality it was just another extract from Ted Harrison's book, *Kriss Akabusi on Track*.

Helping charities is a vexed question for celebrities. The problem is there are so many charities, so many good causes and they all expect the celebrity's support. It is a subject on which Kriss has strong views.

There are certain charities that you work with, and I try to follow the biblical motto of not letting your right hand know what your left hand is doing. In other words, I support charities because I want to help them. I do it quietly without looking for any recognition. I do it because it really means something to me.

People support charities for a variety of reasons. Supporting charities can be wonderful PR. There are some celebrities who seem to be involved in every good cause and you know it is a wonderful way of keeping yourself in the public eye and giving yourself the right image.

I believe that when adopting a charity one should always stay within your own personal interests and decide on your motives. Is it purely to help the charity or is it to make contacts, to earn money or to market your name. When you support a charity, it should be between you and the charity, not something that should be in the public domain.

There are situations where a charity wants Kriss to do something and he says, 'No, thank you.' They come back, 'We really want you and we will pay you.' However, that raises its own problems. If it is a big campaign with a budget which can accommodate a professional fee, OK. However, there are always those people who are ready to criticize the celebrity for taking money from the charity which should really have gone to the good cause.

Kriss's view is that he makes a clear distinction between business and pleasure. If it is business, let him be paid. If it is a charity, it is done for nothing. However, the bottom line is that there are only 24 hours in the day. There is a living to be earned, a family to be seen and only so much one person can do.

In 1996, Kriss was asked to help the British Olympic Association with their fund-raising for Atlanta. He said no, explaining that he had supported such dinners in previous years but that life had moved on. He did not feel that because he had been an Olympian he was obliged to support the cause for the rest of his life.

Of course I have had a relationship with the BOA, but I have also been involved with umpteen other sporting bodies. I earn my living by going to and speaking at dinners like this. That is my business. Surely I cannot be expected to turn up and do my thing free of charge for everyone with whom I have had some association in the past?

On one occasion Kriss declined an invitation to attend a charity fun run event in aid of a national charity. It was a very worthy cause, but he decided that on this occasion it was not possible for him to attend. The charity were not satisfied with this and tried again to persuade him to come. Once more, Kriss politely declined. Shortly afterwards, an article appeared in the Chichester Observer under the headline: 'Akabusi aide shocks Le Jog organisers'. The charity's local fund-raiser, frustrated with Kriss's polite refusal, had decided to throw some mud at Kriss in the local press.

The hub of the matter was the comment of the charity's fund-raiser, 'I wanted someone who was an athlete, a Christian and fairly local. Mr Akabusi fell into all these categories.' That is fair enough. Kriss was, however, disappointed that the charity should have found it necessary to publicize their fun run in a way which portrayed him negatively. A year later, the same charity asked him again to help them!

Kriss goes so many places and meets so many people. It is impossible to remember whom he has met and where he has been. Sometimes, even years later, someone will say thank you for some meeting which has helped them. One such example was the following letter.

Hi Kriss

I really want you to be encouraged in the things you do, especially the small. Roughly 7 or 8 years ago you went to a children's home in Winchester. All the kids made a fuss over you because you were famous except me. I was an angry youth with the kind of problems kids have in care. Despite the bad, deliberate reception I gave you, you managed to break through and showed me the love of God. I'm 21 now and have been born again 2 years. After leaving the kids' home I went back to the street and the crimes of darkness that go on in them – labelled a no-hoper, but then Christ shone his light into my life. I remember finding out you're a born again Christian and God reminded me of that day you came to my children's home. You took me for a little drive up the driveway, let me get out and said 'Jesus loves you' – Now I know!!!
Keep shining!
CU in the Kingdom, love in Christ, Sarah

The day of Kriss Akabusi is a busy day. It is a varied day. If there is time and the schedule permits, Kriss will take Dillinger for a walk (or is it the other way round?). Kriss gives to his new lifestyle the same commitment that he gave to his athletics. It is a day littered with 'Good value!' 'Pump it up!' 'Alrighty, alright!' Sometimes, there are unexpected encouragements, like the letter quoted above. However, there is one thing about which one may be pretty sure, there is a smile on his face. That is something Kriss is comfortable with: 'Part of the fruit of the spirit is joy, and God wants me to express my joy in the best way so people can see you can be a Christian and still have fun.'

And what does the future hold for Kriss Akabusi? This is not a subject about which Kriss loses a lot of sleep. He is happy to live in the present and to remember the words of Jesus: 'Therefore do not worry about tomorrow, for tomorrow will worry about itself. Each day has enough trouble of its own' (Matthew 6:34).

For the moment, he is able to earn a good living just being Kriss Akabusi, and, for the moment, that is enough. He believes, too, that God is in control. Just as he was conscious of God's presence with him in the change of events in 1986 and again at the end of his career, so he can trust God for his future.

How long can he continue in his present role? How long will his popularity last? Who knows? Just one day at a time, just take it as it comes.

Some people have wondered if he might follow Seb Coe into Parliament. Kriss is not so sure: 'I am a political animal but I'm too opinionated. To be in politics, you have to be able to compromise. I am not very good at that.'

Serious TV is another possibility. He would like to diversify his media role. Coaching athletics is also on the cards when the time is right.

Whatever he does, you can be sure he will have fun.

Kriss Akabusi, This is Your Life

1958 28 November – Born in London
1975 7 August – Joins the Army
1982 2 April – Marriage to Monika
1983 5 June – First international, GB v. USSR
       First major championship, World Championships in
       Helsinki
1984 First Olympic Games, Los Angeles. Wins silver medal
       Birth of first daughter, Ashanti
1986 Commonwealth Games and European Championship
       gold medals
1987 First season as hurdler
       13 April – Reaches final in World Championships,
       Rome
       Becomes a Christian
       Birth of second daughter, Shakira
1988 Olympic Games, Seoul
1990 Commonwealth Games and European Championship
       gold medals
       Sets new British record in 400 metres hurdles in
       European Championships final in Split
       November – Leaves the Army

1991 World Championships in Tokyo, bronze and gold medals
      Twice breaks his own British record in the 400 metres hurdles, semi-final and final of World Championships
      Awarded MBE for services to athletics
1992 Olympic Games, Barcelona, two bronze medals
      Breaks his own British record in the 400 metres hurdles, Olympic final
1993 29 August – His last competitive race

Career Summary

Major Championship Medals

1984   Olympic silver medal
      4 × 400m relay

1986   Commonwealth gold medal
      4 × 400m relay
      European Championship gold medal
      4 × 400m relay

1987   World Championship silver medal
      4 × 400m relay

1990   Commonwealth gold medal
      400m hurdles
      European Championship gold medal
      400m hurdles
      European Championship gold medal
      4 × 400m relay

1991   World Championship gold medal
      4 × 400m relay
      World Championship bronze medal
      400m hurdles

Career Summary

1992 Olympic bronze medal
      400m hurdles
      Olympic bronze medal
      4×400m relay

Progress Year by Year

400 metres Flat

Year	Time	UK Ranking
1976	52.4	–
1977	49.1	–
1978	50.2	–
1979	48.7	56th
1980	48.0	32nd
1981	48.0	32nd
1982	48.0	39th
1983	46.10	3rd
1984	45.43	1st
1985	45.55	5th
1986	45.65	6th
1987	45.99	6th
1988	44.93	2nd

400 metres Hurdles

Year	Time	UK Ranking
1987	48.64	1st
1988	48.67	1st
1989	48.59	1st
1990	47.92	1st
1991	47.86	1st
1992	47.82	1st
1993	48.73	1st

Key Races

(Unless otherwise stated, all races 1983–86 are 400 metres flat)

1983

29 May   Edinburgh, UK Championships
2nd 46.85 (PB)

5 June   Birmingham, GB v. USSR
4th 47.65
International debut

18 June   Lappeenranta, GB v. Finland v. Switzerland
1st 46.70 (PB)

24 July   Crystal Palace, AAA Championships
8th 46.81

23 August   Oslo
1st 46.10 (PB)

1984

    28 May Cwmbran, UK Championships
               1st 46.10 (eq. PB)

    6 June Crystal Palace, Olympic trials
               3rd 45.85 (PB)

  4 August LA, Olympic heat
               1st 45.64 (PB)

  5 August LA, Olympic quarter-final
               3rd 45.43 (PB)

  6 August LA, Olympic semi-final
               7th 45.69 (PB)

1985

    4 June Madrid
               1st 45.56

  21 June Birmingham, Eng v. USA
               4th 45.86

  13 July Crystal Palace, AAA Championships heat
               1st 45.55

  14 July Crystal Palace, AAA Championships final
               5th 46.18

1986

  27 April Walnut
               1st 45.74

  26 May Cwmbran, UK Championships
               4th 45.65

  21 June Crystal Palace, AAA Championships
               3rd 46.08

  27 July Edinburgh, Commonwealth final
               4th 46.83

(Unless otherwise stated, all races 1987 onwards are 400 metres hurdles)

1987

16 May	Granada
	2nd 50.16
25 May	Derby, UK Championships
	1st= 49.56 (PB)
20 June	Portsmouth, v. Italy, Czechoslovakia & Bulgaria
	2nd 50.44
10 July	Crystal Palace, Peugeot Talbot
	5th 50.08
17 July	Birmingham, Eng v. USA
	3rd 50.64
2 August	Crystal Palace, AAA 400m flat
	5th 46.13
	(Ran 45.99 in heat)
5 August	La Coruña
	2nd 49.94
14 August	Crystal Palace, IAC
	2nd 49.34 (PB)
30 August	Rome, World Championship heat
	2nd 49.36
31 August	Rome, World Championship semi-final
	3rd 48.64 (PB)
1 September	Rome, World Championship final
	7th 48.74

Career Summary

1988

28 May   San José
           2nd 50.18

24 June   Birmingham, Eng v. USA 400m flat
           1st 46.16

30 June   Helsinki
           1st 49.10

7 August   Birmingham, AAA 400m flat
           1st 44.93 (PB)

17 August   Zurich
           4th 48.67

21 August   Cologne
           2nd 48.89

26 August   Berlin, Grand Prix final
           5th 50.57

23 September   Seoul, Olympic heat
           2nd 49.62

24 September   Seoul, Olympic semi-final
           4th 49.22

25 September   Seoul, Olympic final
           6th 48.69

1989

7 May   Modesto
           3rd 50.15

13 May   Columbus
           2nd 49.99

17 June   Granada
           4th 49.86

20 June   Seville
           3rd 49.04

5 August	Gateshead, Europa Cup	
	1st 48.95	
28 August	Gateshead, Eng v. Ita v. Oceania	
	1st 49.84	
8 September	Barcelona, World Cup	
	3rd 49.42	
13 September	Jerez	
	2nd 48.59 (PB)	

1990

14 January	Sydney	
	1st 49.96	
20 January	Auckland	
	1st 49.03	
28 January	Auckland, Commonwealth heat	
	1st 49.86	
29 January	Auckland, Commonwealth final	
	1st 48.89	
26 May	Granada	
	1st 48.70	
30 May	Seville	
	4th 48.59 (PB)	
3 June	Cardiff, UK Championships	
	1st 51.50	
22 June	Portsmouth, GBR v. USA v. Ken	
	1st 50.10	
29 June	Gateshead, GBR v. GDR v. Can	
	1st 49.22	
26 July	La Coruña	
	4th 48.86	

29 July	New York
	2nd 49.21
7 August	Malmo
	2nd 48.99
9 August	Lahti
	1st 49.38
12 August	Monte Carlo
	1st 48.77
15 August	Zurich
	4th 48.34 (PB)
28 August	Split, European Championship semi-final
	1st 48.84
29 August	Split, European Championship final
	1st 47.92 (PB)
16 September	Sheffield, McVitie's
	1st 50.00

1991

29 June	Europa Cup, Frankfurt
	1st 48.39
12 July	Crystal Palace, Grand Prix
	1st 48.49
19 July	GB v. USSR
	1st 48.79
9 August	Gateshead Invitational
	1st 48.61
25 August	Tokyo, World Championship heat
	1st 48.79
26 August	Tokyo, World Championship semi-final
	1st 47.91 (PB)

27 August   Tokyo, World Championship final
               3rd 47.86 (PB)
15 September Sheffield Invitational
               1st 49.22

1992

2 May   San Diego
          1st 49.85
7 June   Sheffield, UK Championships
          1st 49.00
19 June   Edinburgh, AAA Championships
          1st 49.16
8 July   Lausanne
          3rd, 48.30
10 July   Crystal Palace
          2nd 48.26
6 August   Barcelona, Olympic final
          3rd 47.82 (PB)
16 August   Cologne
          4th 49.07

1993

26 June   Europa Cup, Rome
          4th 48.73
2 July   Meadowbank, TSB Challenge GB v. USA
          1st 50.45
8 August   Monte Carlo, Grand Prix
          6th 49.04
29 August   Sheffield, McDonald's Games
          2nd 49.24.

Career Summary

4 × 400 metres Relay Races

21 August 1983   Crystal Palace, Europa Cup
1st 3:02.28
(Leg 1 in 47.0)

13 August 1983   World Championship heat
3rd 3:10.19

13 August 1983   World Championship semi-final
2nd 3:04.03
GB finished 3rd in final, Akabusi not selected

11 August 1984   Olympic Final
2nd 2:59.13
(Leg 1 in 45.87. European Record)

18 August 1985   Moscow, Europa Cup
3rd 3:03.31

2 August 1986   Commonwealth final
1st 3:07.19
(Leg 1 in 46.8)

31 August 1986   European Championships final
1st 2:59.84
(Leg 2 in 45.2)

6 September 1987 World Championships final
2nd 2:58.86
(Leg 2 in 44.60. European Record)

1 October 1988   Olympic final
5th 3:02.00
(Leg 2 in 44.73)

5 August 1989   Gateshead, Europa Cup
1st 3:03.16
(Leg 2 in 45.4)

8 September 1989	World Cup
	4th 3:02.64
	(Leg 1 in 45.1)
1 September 1990	European Championships
	1st 2:58.22
	(Leg 2 in 44.48. European Record)
1 September 1991	World Championship final
	1st 2:57.53
	(Leg 4 in 44.59. European & Commonwealth record)
8 August 1992	Olympic final
	3rd 2:59.73
26 June 1993	Rome, Europa Cup
	1st 3:00.25.

Ten Things You Never Knew about Kriss Akabusi

1 He has had two dogs, both called Dillinger.
2 He once won a school egg-and-spoon race – he had chewing gum on the spoon.
3 Kriss was the first celebrity to appear on TV's *You Bet* and win nothing for his nominated charity.
4 His car registration is ECC 724, a reminder of Ecclesiastes 7:24, 'What is wisdom? Who can discover it?' (The answer is in Proverbs 9:10, 'The fear of the Lord is the beginning of wisdom'.)
5 He has read the Bible right through every year since 1987.
6 His jockstrap broke during a race – 'It's hard to run flat out with one hand keeping your shorts in place!'
7 His taste in music is Sade or Soul II Soul.
8 He sometimes carries juggling balls with him – 'to show off with. They are great conversation-starters.'
9 He has walked from France to England, via the Channel Tunnel.
10 His house is called '*Laissez faire*'. '*Laissez faire* means for me that when I come through the gates I want to be left alone. Outside the gates I accept that I am public property, but when I come home I want to be able to me myself without being disturbed.'